the
General...
Wishing you love
winds and following
seas... [signature] 2016

JUST BEFORE TAPS

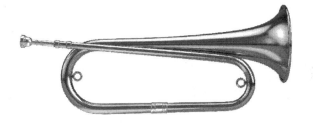

GEORGE WOODRUFF

WITH

RON PAPALEONI, CPO USN RETIRED

PUBLISHED BY LEMON PRESS
ACWORTH, GA
WWW.LEMONPRESSPUBLISHING.COM

Lemon Press Publishing
PO BOX 459
Emerson, GA 30137

www.lemonpresspublishing.com

DEDICATION

Arletha Shanta Boykin Turner, RN
March 21, 1980 to December 26, 2014

The Trinka Davis Veterans Village Community Living Center residents and staff lost a dear friend and a great nurse and Heaven gained an angel!

"See you soon Shanta!"

"Just Before Taps" is dedicated, to the service disabled residents of Trinka Davis Veterans Village, to the wonderful staff of medical professionals, and others, who make our lives more livable and content in what may be for most of us those final days, to the volunteers who give unselfishly of their time and talents to show us they remember, to the American Legion members of the local Posts who have never forgotten us, the Patriot Guard Riders and, especially, to the memory of Trinka Davis and to the officers of the Trinka Davis Foundation she created who made this tribute to those of us who served possible. I know I speak for the residents of Trinka Davis Veterans Village in saying "It is with profound appreciation that we proudly salute you all!"

July, 11, 2014

THE PATRIOT GUARD RIDERS OF GEORGIA, INC. is a non-profit Georgia corporation organized exclusively for charitable and community service to veterans and their families. We have one thing in common, an unwavering respect for those who risk their very lives for America's freedom and security.

Table of Contents

FOREWORD
BY RON PAPALEONI, CPO USN RETIRED

It's the day after Veteran's Day 2015 and it was a fantastic day. I participated in three events; saw many old friends and comrades; watched children and adults waving flags and cheering as we passed them in the Veterans Day Parade in Marietta, Georgia. It's curious that the children were either from private schools or daycare. Veteran's Day is a National Holiday. Banks are closed; governments buildings are closed; there are no municipal services; no postal service and yet our children still have to attend our government schools. But I digress.

After the parade, many of the Patriot Guard Riders rode from Marietta, GA to Kennesaw, GA (about 9 miles) to have lunch. Hundreds of veterans enjoyed a specially prepared meal served by local students. This event was co-sponsored by the City of Kennesaw and American Legion Post 304. After lunch, our bunch kinda split up with many of our veterans going to other events in the area.

Some of us made the jaunt to Acworth, GA for their Veteran's Day celebration at one of the most striking venues around. Patriots Point is located on beautiful Lake Acworth and was specially designed to honor the men and women who served our country. The Chorale Group from North Cobb

Christian School performed and were amazing. The keynote speaker was Cobb County Commissioner, and former Marine, Bob Weatherford who gave a passionate oratory on patriotism.

It was a long and emotional day for all. When I finally got home I had dinner and went to bed early.

The following morning is when it hit me. I got up early and while drinking my coffee got caught up on my emails and social media. There were a good number of posts on FaceBook regarding the Marietta Veterans Day Parade. One that immediately caught my eye was a video of the Patriot Guard Riders (PGR) departing the staging area. The fifty plus Patriots where videoed by Lynn Hubbard, Author and Publisher. Lynn's publishing company is Lemon Press and is responsible for the publishing of this book, "Just Before Taps" by George Woodruff.

Lynn posted the video at 3:01 on November 11, 2015 and the first comment was made at 3:56 by George Woodruff that said, "Thanks. Wish I had been there". Those five words. "Wish I had been there" rang loudly in my ears. As we will learn from this book, George is waiting out his last days in the Trinka Davis Community Living Center. I suddenly realized that George represents the tens of thousands of veterans that are in hospice palliative care. They will, more than likely, not see the next Veteran's Day. They will not be in a parade, or have a veteran appreciation luncheon, or a community celebration to honor them. These veterans sit in VA hospitals, nursing homes, private facilities, and receive very little to honor their service to our country. I'm making a personal commitment to pay more attention to those veterans throughout the year, not just on Veteran's Day.

As you may know, George has given the Patriot Guard Riders of Georgia all rights and profits from this book to be used to expand our Help on the Homefront (HOTH) activities. This assistance can range from helping the wife of a deployed soldier move to another place of residence, to assisting with food and utilities, to building wheelchair ramps for those veterans who have exhausted all other means of support and are in serious need of this service. Visiting VA Hospitals, VA supported nursing homes, and extended care facilities is also high on the HOTH priority list. Just to let them know that we care.

Like George, I believe in the Supreme Architect of the Universe and I know that he sets up "divine appointments" for us. One of those appointments was to meet George Woodruff. The PGR had set up an ice cream social in the Fall of 2014 in memory of one of our most treasured Ride Captains, Lou "Soretoe" Costello. It is always on the third Saturday of the month from 1PM-2PM. That hour is spent serving ice cream and wafer cookies to the residents and *talking* to them; at least for a short period of time.

I'm pretty sure that I meet George on that first day, but I can't be sure. I do remember that in December, I came as Santa to visit and give the vets a small token of our appreciation. The cards and gifts, a PGR Challenge coin had the names of each resident so that we didn't miss anyone. At

2PM we finished and there were a couple of cards left. George's name was on one of them. Our fearless leader, Jerry Green, Crawdaddy, said he would deliver the cards with his grandson Aidyn. Crawdaddy told me later that George was very appreciative and that he was writing a book regarding his final days at Trinka Davis. I would make a point of speaking with him in January.

From that meeting I knew that George was a "standup" kinda guy. Over the next few months, I learned more about his project while talking with the other vets. I loved the interaction with all our veteran residents at Trinka Davis. Their stories are the stuff movies are made from; but better. Men that survived severe wounds, men that were captured and threatened with castration, men that were in the Battle of the Bulge, men ravaged from chemical warfare. These men are from the Army, Navy, Marine Corps, Air Force, Coast Guard, Army Air Corps, Tuskegee Airmen, officers and enlisted men. These men that can no longer walk, talk, eat, hear or breathe without assistance have given their all. They have served during World War II, Korea, Vietnam, Iraq, and Afghanistan. Men that still consider themselves a Band of Brothers. All of them know that they are in the last place they will ever live. Every man dies, but most men do not live a life and have not fought for a cause worth dying for.

At one point, I mentioned that I would like to read a couple of chapters. He sent me all that he had written up to that point. As a retired Navy Chief Petty Officer, I could visualize that barracks at Great Lakes; for I too lived in one at

Camp Perry, at Great Lakes Naval Training Center. I could related to the ups and downs of military life. During my career, I saw many 17 year old boys turn into 18 year old men and squared-away bluejackets. After reading it, I contacted a few friends that were considered to be in the "literary" crowd; sent them a couple of chapters and waited to hear their feedback.

I guess I expected them to get back to me quickly, but alas, that didn't happen. A couple of weeks later, George made the announcement regarding his intent to give the book rights, and profits, to the PGR. Now that kinda lit a fire under me and I got on the horn and told my "literary" friends that I really needed help. Most of their comments were about editing and publishing.

Then IT happened. You know that little voice that speaks to you from time to time? Well, the voice was getting louder and clearer. "Pappy," the voice said, "your answer is right in front of you." Sometimes the voice calls me Pappy, or Ron, or Dummy, or other words of endearment. But again, I digress.

Lynn Hubbard is an author AND a publisher. She had already asked me to be a contributor to her latest book "PTSD-No Apologies", a compilation of short stories and poetry told through the eyes of those that have been through much trauma. We talked and decided to proceed with the book, "Just Before Taps". We passed our suggestions on to the PGR of Georgia State Captain Jeff "JayDub" Goodiel and received his approval. All the proper documents were signed and as George would say, "We're off to the races."

I had more than a little experience editing technical documents, executive summaries and presentations, so I told Lynn that I would edit the manuscript when it was completed. I did not know at the time but all my experience in editing didn't mean squat. I promised George that when editing the manuscript, I would not change his words. Just Before Taps is written as a journal in the first person. It's George's recollection of both recent and past events. The words he uses are written in the vernacular of his generation and may seem out of date. However, I refused to change them.

Punctuation, on the other hand, was something else. For example: As a writer, who has experienced the friendship, love, and warmth, of another human being, I still am amazed that peace, love, and pizza can be bought, not only online, but in the store. George did not write that but after the first couple of hours, I went into a comma coma. During this early editing time, George completed the last chapter and we were still a long away from publishing.

In July, Lynn and I had played Ping-Pong with the manuscript and George's health was beginning to worsen, so we decided to present George with a bound copy of the manuscript at the Ice Cream Social in July. He was ecstatic. His spirits rose and we thought we were getting close to final publication.

Not so fast Buckaroo. We still needed photos and a final cover for Just Before Taps. George wanted his family and close friends to see his work while he still could sign a copy. Through her publishing company, Lemon Press, Lynn had a limited number of the manuscript put into a soft cover book. George couldn't have been happier.

George is a miracle and we treasure every moment he's with us. However, his health is again failing. His nightly pain meds put him out for 10 hours. He recently made another trip to the VA Medical Center in Atlanta to find out why he was retaining so much water. After a few days, the VA sent him back to Trinka Davis and placed him in palliative care. Palliative care is a discipline that provides patients with relief from the symptoms of any serious illness. It's designed to give patients a better quality of life. George is already in Hospice so Palliative care is that little extra that keeps you going.

So while I was writing this missive, I get an email from George telling me that he has already written 12,000 words in his NEW book, "My Time to Die" with one finger typing. The man is incredible!!! It's obvious that God has not finished using George Woodruff.

During the past year, I've learned a lot from George. He's encouraged me to finish a book that I started four years ago, he has taught me the value of "pressing on" no matter what, he has instilled a feeling of power that I can do anything if I focus on it.

He's my Shipmate, my Masonic Brother, and over the past year, my Mentor and Friend.

So I invite you to read the book and share it with others. George's greatest wish is for this book to make a difference. To encourage others to build facilities that rival Trinka Davis. To let our vets, who have given so much, live a peaceful and joyful life. It can be done.

INTRODUCTION

This is the story of how Trinka Davis Veterans Village came into being, the story of the seriously service disabled veterans who live in the Community Living Center, and the story of the wonderful staff of doctors, nurses, nursing assistants, and other health and service personnel who take care of them. It is an unusual story because Veterans Village is "one of a kind"." It was built entirely with private money given by Trinka Davis to the Trinka Davis Foundation that bears her name and donated to the Veterans Administration when completed.

Trinka Davis died unexpectedly, in 2006, before she could see her dream come to fruition. Despite the fact that she was no longer with them to see it through, the officers of the Trinka Davis Foundation she had created carried out her wishes to help the veterans she cared so much. Hopefully, what they did so well will provide the model that will encourage other patriotic individuals of means to participate in building similar Veterans Villages across this nation. That way, veterans who have paid a high price for their service in various wars will be able to receive the quality of care they deserve.

Let's start the book by explaining how Trinka Davis Veterans Village Community Living Center came into being. I also feel the need to explain how wounds and injuries incurred in the military often come with the need for longtime medical care, including the kind this outstanding Community Living Center provides to its residents. I will try to do this by telling you my own personal story of how an accident that happened to me, while serving in the U.S. Navy, during World War II, affected my entire life and eventually qualified me to become a resident of this amazing place.

It is hard to adequately describe the amazing 48,000 square foot 44 bed Trinka Davis Veterans Village Community Living Center which takes up the major portion of the magnificent 73,900 square foot structure. It was designed by Peacock Partnership, an Atlanta architectural firm specializing in healthcare design and built by R. K. Redding Construction. It admitted its first resident in early February, 2013. How the well thought out planning of the Community Living Center has worked to improve the lives of its disabled veteran residents will become crystal clear as "Just Before Taps" goes on to tell a most amazing story that could not have happened except for the caring of Trinka Davis and the Foundation she created. The remainder of the building is designed as a fully equipped and staffed 25,900 square foot Veterans Administration Outpatient Clinic that serves thousands of local veterans as well as the residents of the Community Living Center. The Clinic, which opened in late September, 2012, offers services including primary care, home based primary care, internal medicine, mental health, podiatric care, vision care, dental care, physical and occupational therapy, radiology, audiology, and other visiting specialists. It also offers tele-medicine through the latest technology in video teleconferencing. High quality medical care that formerly required area veterans to make long trips along an often packed interstate highway to Atlanta Veterans Administration Medical Center (VAMC) is now available nearer to their homes. God Bless Trinka Davis whose generosity and deep concern for the medical needs of the veterans who proudly served and sacrificed led her to create and fund The Trinka Davis Foundation that made this possible! Well done, Trinka. May you forever rest in peace!

After a lot of thought, I concluded that a fitting title for my book would be "Just Before Taps"." While it may raise a few eyebrows, its meaning is abundantly clear to those who have served our country in the military. Every evening, when day is done, the flag is lowered and the mournful sound of Taps resounds across our military installations. When a veteran passes on, and chooses a military funeral, often with a Committal Service, Taps is sounded to signify that the veteran's work is finished and he or she has earned eternal rest. Many of us who live at Trinka Davis Veterans Village CLC (myself included) will probably spend the rest of our days right here until we finally earn the eternal rest that eventually comes to all mankind. Hence the title "Just Before Taps"."

"Just Before Taps" is dedicated, to the service disabled residents of Trinka Davis Veterans Village, to the wonderful staff of medical professionals, and others, who make our lives more livable and content in what may be for most of us those final days, to the volunteers who give unselfishly of their time and talents to show us they remember, to the American Legion members of the local Posts who have never forgotten us, the Patriot Guard Riders and, especially, to the memory of Trinka Davis and to the officers of the Trinka Davis Foundation she created who made this tribute to those of us who served possible. I know I speak for the residents of Trinka Davis Veterans Village in saying "It is with profound appreciation that we proudly salute you all!"

July, 11, 2014

CHAPTER ONE

Moving Day

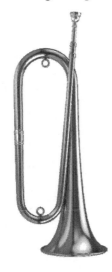

Wednesday, May 15, 2014, was a sad day. Perhaps the saddest day of, what had been for my sweet wife Jeanne and I, a long and very happy marriage. This was the day I had been dreading. Jeanne and I would no longer be living together. We were both in our eighties and time had caught up with us. My service-connected disability worsened and along with the ravages of old age, my health had failed, Jeanne had developed memory problems over the years. We had finally reached the point where we could no longer take care of ourselves or each other. We made our decision and we would have to try to live with it. There was no turning back,

Today we would be leaving our Canton condominium, in lovely Riverstone Villas, never to return. From this day forward, I would be living at Trinka Davis Veterans Village Community Living Center, in Carrollton, Georgia. Jeanne would be moving to Emeritus Riverstone Assisted Living in Canton, where she would get the care she needed, and where our daughter, Julie Shannon, could look out for her. We waited silently...fearing the moment when Julie would pull her Toyota into our condo's short driveway and pick us up for the beginning leg of our last journey together.

Our first destination would be Trinka Davis Veterans Village. Our son-in-law Tom, and our grandson Cory, had loaded my belongings in their van the night before so we could get an early start. During the past week Jeanne's small apartment at Emeritus Riverstone had been prepared for her move with help from my daughter Sandra and our other son-in-law (also named Tom).They had come up from Tallahassee to help move some of the heavier furniture to Jeanne's new apartment. so that way it would be ready for her when she arrived. All in all this was a family affair. We were very proud of our children and no one ever was blessed with better sons-in-law.

I had first learned about the existence of Trinka Davis Veterans Village Community Living Center when my VA psychologist, Dr. Regina Sherman, suggested it was time for me to consider it. With the aid of the Atlanta VA's Bronze Clinic's Social Worker, Mrs. Lerch, we had made a trip to Trinka Davis Veterans Village Community Living Center a few weeks before to look it over. When we arrived we were met by Jennifer Talley an attractive young Clinical Social Worker with a sweet disposition and an understanding manner. We were given the "cooks tour" and discovered the center to be almost beyond belief. This was no ordinary nursing home! It was "one of a kind" as the reader will discover as the story continues.

A couple of weeks prior to my move to Trinka Davis Veterans Village, I had what turned out to be my final appointment with my primary care physician, Dr. Rina Eisenstein at the Atlanta VA Medical Center's Bronze Clinic. We had developed a great doctor/patient relationship over the five years she had treated me and, in my opinion, she could almost walk on water. I told her of my plan to move my wife Jeanne, to assisted living. She told me that I could not live alone. With the help of the Social Worker, Mrs. Lerch, arrangements were made for me to be admitted to Trinka Davis on May 15, 2014.

Time flew by quickly as my daughter, Julie and I made arrangements for Jeanne's move to Emeritus Riverstone Assisted Living with our cat, Snoopy. Snoopy loved Jeanne and we knew she would provide much needed companionship to make Jeanne's adjustment to her new home a bit easier. Everything had been completed, the day of departure had arrived, as Julie pulled out of our driveway, I took a quick last look at the condo we had been sharing for more than two years since moving to Canton from Mineral Bluff., Mineral Bluff is nestled in the beautiful north Georgia mountains, just a few miles north of the small city of Blue Ridge. It was a two bedroom, two bath, villa type in a well-kept 82 unit location with a clubhouse, pool, library, and exercise room. We had purchased it when prices were down. We had installed new carpet, stainless steel kitchen appliances, and other improvements and, as we owned it free and clear, we should

3

make a nice profit on it. The money from the sale would be deposited in the bank and, along with the considerable savings we had accumulated, should take care of Jeanne's security for many years. Knowing we had no financial concerns took a heavy load off our minds. Our main problem would be adjusting to our change in lifestyle and the fact that we would no longer be together after so many years of marriage.

About 9:30 am we heard Julie pull into the driveway. I had a lump in my throat that felt as big as a baseball, and I could hardly choke back the tears that were welling up in my eyes as we got into her car to begin the 70 mile trip from Canton to Carrollton. I felt like I was dying inside but I knew there was no other choice than the one we had reluctantly made.

Everything was quiet in the big car as it hummed along the crowded Interstate highway toward its destination in Carrollton. I sat in the front with Julie. My wife, Jeanne, and my grandson Cory occupied the back seat. There was little conversation as everyone seemed to be lost in their own thoughts. As the miles flew by my thoughts began to take a turn from the problems of the present to the memories of days gone by. Past events that had occurred during my long life flew vividly before me. Memories both good and bad filled my mind. Memories that had finally led up to today.

CHAPTER TWO

Navy Blues

Suddenly, it was 1944 again. I was that boy from Akron, Ohio, who had just turned seventeen. WWII was at its peak with fighting in both Europe and the Pacific theater. In my mind it was a battle for freedom as opposed to tyranny and I wanted to be a part of it. I was too young to enlist without parental consent so I worked on my father until he agreed to sign for me. On August 8, 1944 I enlisted and on September 5th I was sent to Boot Camp at Camp Downes, Great Lakes Naval Training Center.

As anyone who has been through it can tell you, Boot Camp in those days was no picnic! It was "march...march...march" on the grinder until you thought your legs would fall off. It was being ordered to don a gas mask; enter a large chamber where they filled it with tear gas. You were then ordered to remove your gas mask while still inside. When it was off you choked...tears ran down your face...and just when you thought you could not stand anymore you were ordered to replace your gas mask. Wow! You could breathe again! Boot Camp was tough but you learned to follow

1

orders that might keep you alive when the shooting started and where boys, myself included, became men.

The winter of 1944-45 at Great Lakes was cold enough  to freeze the ears off a brass monkey! It was also the time of the Scarlet Fever epidemic. It spread like wildfire across the length and breadth of the Great Lakes Naval Training Center. Huge numbers of naval personnel in the Boot Camps came down with it, myself included. We were hospitalized and quarantined for 21 days in long, open wards that held 30 or more beds. All of us in my Ward champed at the bit wanting to get out and join the fight. Since we were mostly untried "Boots" we had no idea of what war was like.

When I finally graduated from Boot Camp I was assigned to go to Basic Engineering School and temporarily transferred to the Replacement Depot, at Great Lakes, to await transfer to the base where the school was located. It was a large building jammed with triple decker bunks that rested on a concrete floor. I was assigned to the very top bunk which put me some eight feet above the floor level. The bunk was narrow with no side rails. For me it was an accident waiting to happen. And it sure did!

One morning I awoke finding myself lying face down on the concrete floor in a pool of blood. My nose was broken, which accounted for the blood, plus I had a few scrapes and sore spots. When the fall had happened and how long I had lain there on the concrete was anybody's guess. Could have been minutes; could have been longer. With a little help from a nearby sailor I got up off the floor and headed for the Aid Station feeling like a fool.

The medical corpsman on duty straightened my nose; taped it into position; attended to my scrapes and sent me on my merry way. I (and probably he) had no idea of how serious my injuries from the fall actually were. I was to find this out the hard way over many years as the problems caused by the fall worsened and medical knowledge slowly progressed.

Since this had happened to me years before the advent of CT scanners and MRI's little was known about Traumatic Brain Injuries or the lifelong medical problems they could cause in some cases. Left untreated, Traumatic Brain Injuries can cause seizures, mood swings, and other problems which were, at the time, hard to diagnose and difficult to treat. And, as time went by, that is what happened to me.

Like most 17 year olds, I thought I was invincible and ignored the problems that began after the fall. I was transferred from Great Lakes to the U.S. Naval Advance Base Personnel Depot at what was formerly Tanforan Race Track in San Bruno, California. There I underwent 16 weeks of

Advanced Training that consisted of the use of Judo in hand to hand combat, extensive practice on the rifle range, and hikes as far as 40 miles with 80 pound packs. I began to wonder if I had somehow been transferred to the Marine Corps! At the time I didn't understand the purpose of this extensive training. As the days passed I found out.

During my stay at San Bruno there is an incident I recall that in retrospect was kind of funny. We were assigned to live in wooden barracks that held a couple of dozen men, twelve to a side, with a table in the middle that served as a place to play cards and gather for the usual bull sessions that are a part of military life. With so many men sleeping in a small area every sound and smell was noticeable.

We had among us one slightly overweight sailor who was not too clean. He emitted a strong odor at night as he rarely bathed. One particular night we simply could not stand the smell. Somebody yelled out "Let's give 'Fats' a GI bath"." We arose as one man; grabbed him; and hustled him about a half block down the concrete walkway that separated the various barracks from the shower and toilet facilities. With a stiff brush and soap we hauled his carcass into the shower and scrubbed him until his skin was red. From that time on "Fats" was the cleanest guy in the barracks.

It was during this 16 week training period that problems from my fall, at Great Lakes began to manifest themselves. I would have periods of extreme irritability and occasional blank spots in my memory that I could not account

4

for. Being a 17 year old with a macho attitude, I just put it down to being worn out from long, hard, days and shrugged it off.

When the training was over, I was transferred to the U.S. Naval Net Depot, at Tiburon, California.

One of the Net Depot's functions was to tend to the huge nets whose purpose was to stop enemy torpedoes and

5

submarines from entering San Francisco Bay. The Net Depot also was home to a number of small landing craft, including LCVP's. For those who may not understand what the initials signify, an LCVP is a Landing Craft Vehicle Personnel (also known as a Higgins boat) whose job is to carry troops and small vehicles from larger craft, such as troop carriers, to invasion points on the beach. Tough job for both the troops and the operator of the LCVP as the enemy's bullets and heavy guns are usually firing at you all the way. Many of these crafts, especially those used in the "D-Day" invasion and South Pacific island invasions, never made it to shore.

One of my duties while stationed at the Net Depot was to occasionally operate a "liberty launch" from Tiburon (which was located on the Bay at the tip of a peninsula) to San Francisco where the sailors on pass disembarked for a good time in the city. "'Nuff said about that!"

I remember some of the fun times we had while at Tiburon including the time when I picked up a jellyfish from the ocean and placed it on the mattress of a fellow sailor's bunk. When he got back from liberty after having "one too many" he slept on it all night and didn't discover it until the next morning. He was one angry sailor...hangover and all. Fortunately, the jellyfish wasn't the poisonous type and I never got caught. The problems from the fall continued to persist and, as I didn't understand it, I continued to ignore it.

After serving at the Net Depot for a few months, I was transferred to the Naval Landing Force Equipment Depot in

Albany, California. The Equipment Depot, formerly a race track, was used for storing hundreds of landing craft for use in the Pacific plus a lot of repair parts including rows of large Grey Marine Diesel Engines. I didn't know it at the time but what happened at the Equipment Depot would lead to the end of my naval career.

By then I had been promoted to Fireman First Class and one of my duties there was to operate a fork lift to transport heavy parts from one location to another. Everything went along fine until one day while driving the fork lift I blacked out. I went over the edge of a wall and crashed down unto a large diesel engine a few feet below. The Lieutenant on duty started to raise Cain with me until he realized that I apparently had some kind of a medical problem. I was sent to Oakland Naval Hospital for evaluation and treatment.

Oakland Naval Hospital (also known as Oak Knoll) was located in Oakland, California, and had opened in 1942 for the treatment of military personnel who had been wounded or otherwise disabled in the Pacific theater. It was huge and able to provide medical care for thousands and there were plenty of casualties from the battles to retake the Pacific islands from the Japanese to keep it full to capacity.

After being examined, the doctors could not decide what was wrong with me. They believed it must be some kind of a nervous condition so they placed me in an open psychiatric ward with a lot of sailors and Marines who had been shipped back from the Pacific. Most had been through unimaginable hell in the thick of the fighting during the invasions of numerous Pacific islands. It was there that I got my first look at the horror of what we now identify as PTSD and the lifelong disabilities that can result from it. I will never forget it as long as I live.

I was in the hospital for only a short time when Japan finally agreed to surrender on August 14, 1945. Atom bombs had been dropped on Hiroshima (Little Boy) on August 6th and on Nagasaki (Fat Man) on August 9th devastating both Japanese cities and killing untold thousands. But as horrible as it was an invasion of the Japanese homeland could have killed millions and devastated the infrastructure of the nation. Amphibious units such as the one I had served in would have been ordered to storm Japanese beaches with LCVP's carrying hundreds of thousands of soldiers and Marines. Casualty rates would have been enormous for our military, the Japanese military, and Japanese civilians. I will always be grateful for President Harry Truman and for the decision he made to drop those bombs. It ended the war!

Early on the morning of August 15, 1945, at Oakland Naval Hospital, the victory celebration in my hospital Ward got underway full blast! The sailors and Marines shouting, slapping each other on the back, shaking hands, and generally whooping it up. The war was over! No more fighting. No invasion of the Japanese mainland with heavy casualties on both sides. We could all go home at last!

But across the Bay in San Francisco, it was a far different story. What began as a "Victory Celebration" had turned into the deadliest "riot" in the city's history! The riot was mostly confined to downtown San Francisco and involved thousands of intoxicated soldiers and sailors along with a substantial number of the city's residents. Shamefully, it turned out that San Francisco was the only city in the United States that celebrated "victory" with a "riot"." On September 2, 1945, Japan officially surrendered. The Formal Surrender Document was signed aboard the Battleship Missouri near Tokyo, Japan, officially ending World War II.

Twenty seven days later, on September 29, 1945, I received my Honorable Discharge from the U.S. Navy for medical reasons. I was awarded a ten percent service-connected disability for "anxiety" and zero percent for "hemorrhoids"." Kind of a "top to bottom" case, I guess. I had served my country for a year and twenty four days and I was just eighteen years old.

My fall from the top of a triple decker bunk to a concrete floor, at Great Lakes, to the best of my recollection, was never considered or discussed with the Navy hospital's doctors. I knew nothing about Traumatic Brain Injuries and the potential future problems they could cause. At the time I just wanted to go home. For me the war was over. It was time to start living. I had no idea of how the severe problems from the fall, at Great Lakes, would affect me in the future. And, at that time, neither did the doctors. As time passed, we would

9

both find out.

Honorable Discharge in hand, loaded sea bag slung across my left shoulder, and the "ruptured duck" that was given to honorably discharged veterans pinned to my navy blouse, I boarded the train in San Francisco for an "across the country" trip to Akron, Ohio. I was assigned an upper berth in a Pullman Car. During the day, the upper was pushed up out of sight while the lower berth became seats that could hold four people. As the son of a railroader, I enjoyed the sound of the train's wheels clicking on the rails and watching the landscape flowing by. I always tried to get the window seat. One memory that sticks in my mind is admiring the beautiful green pastures as we rolled through Iowa. When we finally arrived in Akron I detrained and my mom and dad were there waiting for me. It was so good to be home or so I thought. It turned out that my parents had decided to sell their house by the lake and retire to a Mobile Home Park, in St. Petersburg, Florida. Oh, well!

A short time after leaving the Navy and returning to civilian life, I began to again have problems with irritability, depression, and short blank periods in my memory. I didn't know what was wrong with me so in 1946 I went to Crile Veterans Hospital in Parma, Ohio near Cleveland, for treatment. I was admitted and hospitalized for several weeks. The hospital was a former Army hospital that opened in 1943 and, in addition to the patients it served, it also had housed some 300 German prisoners of war plus a few Italians.

The various patient wards were made up of wooden barracks type structures. There were no private rooms like you see in today's Veterans Medical Centers. Patients occupied "side by side" hospital beds in long rows on both sides of a ward and individual privacy was something that was unknown. It was kind of primitive but adequate for the purposes it served.

After spending several weeks as an "inpatient", at Crile Veterans Hospital, without any real improvement in my condition, I was discharged. Again, neither I, nor the doctors who treated me, discussed my fall at Great Lakes. That the problems I was having could be traced to a simple fall from a triple decker bunk to a concrete floor seemed improbable back in 1946. My parents had already moved to Florida and I needed work. I took a temporary job at Crile as a nursing assistant. And "temporary" was what it turned out to be. I soon discovered I wasn't suited for hospital work, quit the job, and moved to St. Petersburg to live with my folks. I was nineteen years old.

For me, St. Petersburg in 1946, was a most unusual city. Now that the war was over, and the military had left, it was beginning to fill up with retirees. Green benches, everywhere in the downtown area, were filled with tourists and local folks basking in the sun and watching the world go by. There were old streetcars filled with people that swayed from side to side as they rambled along their routes and the Municipal Pier that extended far out into the Bay. If the sun

11

failed to shine one of the daily papers gave away an entire issue. In the center of "downtown" Williams Park covered several square blocks and had a bandstand in the center of the park where folks sat in benches to watch the goings on. Lots to do back in 1946...even for a nineteen year old Navy veteran.

One other exceptional attraction was a large retail outlet with several floors called Webb's City. It was located on Ninth Street, just off Central Avenue and bore the title of "The World's Most Unusual Drug Store"." It sold everything imaginable and even sported a large Barber Shop that offered haircuts for the magnificent sum of thirty five cents.

My dad and I used to go there often as it was the cheapest place in town. When the barber had finished scalping you, (in about three minutes flat) you were handed a coupon that allowed you to purchase a "double dip" ice cream cone from Webb's City for a nickel. Gas for your car was about nineteen cents per gallon and chuck roast was just nineteen cents a pound. The owner of this unusual place "Doc Webb" was a real showman and the title "The World's Most Unusual Drug Store" fit it to a tee.

As I hadn't finished high school when I enlisted in the Navy, I decided to take a General Educational Development test at St. Petersburg Senior High School. I passed it with a ninety five percentage point average and was awarded my diploma. I didn't feel much like going to work right away so I joined something called the "52-20" club. When you got out of the service you could get a check for twenty dollars for up to fifty two weeks...hence the name. You simply signed up at the State Employment Office and, while you were supposed to looking for a job, you went by each week and picked up your twenty bucks. Doesn't sound like much now but those days twenty dollars went a long way.

As my mother and father lived in a rather small mobile home, and as my presence crowded them a bit, I decided to move. The place I choose was a boarding house operated by a semi-sweet little old lady we called Granny Raley. She charged most of her boarders twelve dollars a week but, because of my rather healthy appetite and my speed at the table, I was charged thirteen. That left me with seven dollars each week to meet my other needs.

Granny Raley's southern style cooking was pretty good. She made a biscuit type "hoe cake" in a large frying pan and cut it into large, wedge shaped pieces. It was delicious! While I got my hand gently slapped by her more than once trying to get a second piece more often than not I got away with it. When Granny thought supper's roast might be a little tough she would remark to all of us within listening distance. "'At's a tough old bull" in her delightful southern drawl. And sometimes it was.

After living at Granny's boarding house for a few weeks I came to the conclusion that I needed to get a job. Before joining the Navy, I had worked summers at Goodyear Aircraft for a friend of my dad's and later as an apprentice electrician for Firestone Tire and Rubber Company. After some unsuccessful job hunting, I took a job with Florida Power on the "GI Bill" to train to build power substations. I continued to have problems with depression, irritability, and short periods of time that were missing from my memory. The job was dangerous as it required a lot of climbing and working with heavy tools to fasten steel girders together.

Eventually, I realized it was simply too dangerous for someone with my problems. I gave up the job, packed my clothes, and got on my Royal Enfield motorcycle to tour the country. The motorcycle gave up the ghost in Biloxi, Mississippi and it was junked. From then on I was "hitchhiking" to get to my chosen destination and that is what I did. I had some interesting experiences on the road that I will never forget. I remember working in the oil fields, in Texas, picking cherries outside Sunnyvale, California and working as an electrician, wiring houses in Reno, Nevada. Those were the good times.

I also remember sleeping in jail cells in various towns across the country overnight, with the consent of the town's police chief, and the promise of moving on in the morning. Sometimes the jail came with breakfast and sometimes not. I also stopped at a number of Salvation Army shelters where you could get bed and breakfast and maybe a bath. One night, outside El Paso, Texas, a veteran buddy I had met on the road and I slept in a draw under the highway. During the night, we were approached by a curious coyote. I was startled as I had no experience with the furry critters and asked my friend if he had. He answered "just shut up and go to sleep. It's only a "mangy coyote"." I covered myself up with old newspapers against the night's chill and sleep I did.

Time went by and I was a mess. I didn't understand what the matter with me was and I had no idea how to fix it. I guess I was a "road bum" for the better part of a year. Didn't like it and couldn't seem to change it. So I just kept on traveling from state to state until one day in September 1947, I stopped in Houston, Texas. After spending the night in a Salvation Army shelter I cleaned up, had a good breakfast and decided to look the big city over.

While walking around Houston's downtown area I met a Sergeant in Army uniform. We talked. At some point, during our conversation, he informed me he was an Army recruiter. When he learned I had served in the Navy, he invited me to come down to his office, where he had a small bar, and share a beer or two with him. I did. We "chewed the fat" as folks who have served in the military often do and after a couple of beers, he asked me to take a test just to see how high I could score on it. I agreed to humor him as he was providing the beer and my thirst hadn't been fully quenched. He graded the test and informed me I had made an exceptionally high score and could easily qualify for a branch of Army intelligence.

I knew I had a service-connected disability from the Navy, rated at ten percent, and showed him the front of my discharge paper which indicated it was an Honorable Discharge. I don't recall if he looked at the back which

15

indicated I had been discharged for "medical reasons"."

Anyway, the beer kept flowing and the company was excellent. When I woke up the next morning I was on a train to Fort Ord, California. Somehow, I had joined the U.S. Army!

CHAPTER THREE

Army Days

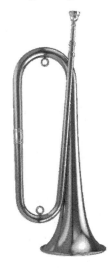

When I arrived at Fort Ord, California in late September 1947. The U.S. Army post was located on the Pacific Coast at Monterey Bay. Considered by some to be the most beautiful post in the United States, it covered over 28,000 acres. Its climate supposedly consisted of warm, dry summers and cool, rainy winters. What the local boosters failed to tell us incoming GI's was that summer days could hit 100 degrees or more and the dust kicked up by your combat boots during a long march was enough to choke a camel!

In 1946, Fort Ord had become a training facility for basic combat and advance infantry training. In July 1947, it had become home to the 4th Replacement Training Center and the 4th Infantry Division, which had been reactivated and had also taken up residence at the fort. "What has that fast talking, beer drinking, Recruiting Sergeant, in Houston gotten me into?" I asked myself. And when I discovered that I would have to undergo six weeks of tough "refresher" training before being reassigned to another base I almost blew a gasket! To make matters even worse it was wooden barracks again with smelly soldiers sleeping head to toe.

Actually, despite my grumbling, my time at Fort Ord turned out better than I had hoped and before "refresher" training was complete I decided I really liked the Army. Fort Ord was located about 340 miles north of Los Angeles, roughly 100 miles south of San Francisco, and just a few minutes from Monterey, Pacific Grove, and Carmel. Salinas was about 14 miles and Watsonville a little further. While I visited them all, I liked Carmel (aka Carmel by the Sea) best. Gorgeous scenery, nice restaurants, friendly people, and just about everything a 20 year old soldier could want.

Refresher training complete, I was transferred to Vint Hill Farms Station near Warrenton, Virginia. There were a couple of hundred of us trainees there at the time, plus numerous Military Police guarding the base. Naturally, it was wooden barracks again, but this time with "potbellied stoves" which we continually stoked with hardwood to try to keep warm. The place was ankle deep in red clay mud and heavily populated with squirrels who spent most of their time raiding hickory nut trees to add to their dwindling winter supplies.

Vint Hill Farms Station was the first field station of the Army Security Agency, a subordinate to the National Security Agency (NSA). The facility conducted signal intelligence operations and was a training center for cryptologists, radio intercept operators, and radio repair technicians. The goal of Vint Hill Farms Station was to eavesdrop on any transmission, decode it and relay the information gained to government officials in Washington, D.C. In October of 1946, it was designated as the Army Security Agency School.

When I got there in late 1947, Vint Hill Farms was kind of in the middle of nowhere and, outside of training, there really wasn't much to do. Everywhere you went, even to town on pass, you had to wear a little rope around your neck from which dangled a card encased in clear plastic, about the size of a pack of cigarettes. If I remember correctly the card was

19

sort of orange colored and had a capital letter on it that apparently designated something. I never did figure out what but "scuttlebutt" had it that the card identified you as a branch of Army Intelligence. If you were in the military you knew enough to take "scuttlebutt" with a grain of salt.

I do know that there were about as many guards around the post as there were trainees in the School and you needed a "top secret" clearance to be there. When my dad called me to ask what kind of trouble I was in to he told me that the FBI, the CIC, local authorities, and gosh knows who else had been around asking our neighbors in Florida questions about me. It was then it was discovered I had a Medical Discharge from the Navy. I was asked if I wanted out of the Army. I told them "No" and that I liked the Army. Nothing more was ever said to me about the subject.

One of our major sources of fun at Vint Hill was playing football. For us, it was a "rough and tumble" sport with no holds barred. I played Center and frequently got dumped on my backside by the over enthusiastic opposition. I will always remember one particular game in early 1948, where I got smacked from both sides because it put me in Fort Belvoir Station Hospital with an injured left knee. After a few days of hobbling around I was transferred to an orthopedic ward at Walter Reed Army Hospital in Washington, D.C.

When I got discharged from Walter Reed I was transferred from Vint Hill Station to Headquarters and Headquarters Company, Third Army at Fort Benning near

Columbus, Georgia. I wanted to go to the Military Academy at West Point to get a good education with the idea of a military career. I took the written examination to see if I could qualify for the Prep School and passed easily. Then came the physical exam and I flunked. The reason given for my failure was that I had second degree 'pes planus"." In short...I had "flat feet"! Since I had scored well on the written test I was urged by my Commanding Officer to apply for Officer's Candidate School. I considered it but in the end I decided to turn it down.

It was probably best for both me and the Army that I decided against OCS. The medical issues that had begun to affect me, after my fall while serving in the Navy at Great Lakes from the top of that three decker bunk, were still causing problems. Eventually, I ended up as a patient at Fort Benning Station Hospital. After a short time, I was transferred to Oliver General Hospital in Augusta for treatment that wasn't available at Fort Benning. Oliver General was a beautiful place. It offered lots of activities to do for those of us who were ambulatory. One of them was horseback riding. I knew little or nothing about horses. Not wanting to show my ignorance, I picked what appeared to be a gentle old beast and, with a little help, I climbed aboard. My mistake. And it was a big one!

As we were plodding slowly along a tree lined path one of the more skillful riders near the lead urged his horse into a gallop. "Old Dobbin", as I called my mount, did his best to follow, panting and wheezing like a worn out steam engine with each stride. I tried to evade a large branch hanging over the path and failed miserably. I was knocked off the old fellow and with my right foot caught in the stirrup, was hauled over a pile of rocks at full tilt! Battered, bruised, and the subject of much joshing, I eventually recovered. My medical record put it down "as a second case of head trauma"." It happened in 1948 and I have never been on a horse since.

After I was released as a patient, I did temporary duty at Oliver General Hospital while waiting for assignment to my next duty station. Mostly, it consisted of doing guard duty at night by walking around a large building that covered about a square block. It could be kind of scary. There was a big, dark, woods on the back side and wide open space on the other three sides. We had no weapon for protection other than a small club about a foot long. What good it could have done in case it was needed was beyond me. I never discovered what was in the building I was supposed to be guarding but, since nothing much ever happened, I came to believe it was just a "make work" job. The Army does that to you now and then.

Finally, my orders came. I was transferred to Camp Kilmer New Jersey and pegged for overseas duty in Germany. Camp Kilmer was not far from New York City. Whenever I got a pass, I jumped at the chance to ride the train to the "Big Apple"." Things were quite expensive there and, as a buck private, my funds were kind of limited. I usually walked around and gawked at the huge, towering, skyscrapers and occasionally ate a delicious hotdog purchased from a vendor with a pushcart. "New York...New York"! It was really a grand sight to a kid from the boonies!

At last the big day came. We were shipping out and assigned to a "troop ship", the General Maurice Rose, bound for Bremerhaven, Germany. We were scheduled for arrival there on the 7th or 8th of April, 1949. The General Rose was 800 feet long, 80 feet wide, and had just been remodeled. It was by far the largest ship I had ever been on. Most of my Navy service had been with LCVP's, except for one short trip on a net tender when I had been at Tiburon. During World War II, the General Rose had carried 5000 troops at a time. On this voyage it would be traveling light with only 800 of us aboard. The sea was smooth as glass all the way and the weather was beautiful.

On April 4, 1949, the crew of the General Rose held a raucous event in which all of us who were headed for Germany were made members of the Royal Order of Atlantic Voyageurs. While it was somewhat boisterous and loud, none of us had to walk the plank and it was pure fun! We were awarded fancy certificates signed by the Royal Navigator and Royal Chamberlain for Headquarters Atlantic Sector, Kingdom of the Briny Deep. It was a big joke but it broke up the monotony of the long voyage. One other thing about the voyage that will always remain in my memory was the trip through the English Channel and seeing the White Cliffs of Dover, on the English side. It was an awesome sight and a "jaw dropper" for a twenty one year old from the sticks! When the General Maurice Rose docked at Bremerhaven we went ashore lugging our heavy footlockers stuffed with everything we owned. With little delay, we were loaded onto a train headed straight for Marburg.

These were difficult times in Germany. It was hard to tell what the future held for those of us who would serve in the Army of Occupation. The Soviet Union's land blockade of Berlin had been imposed by Stalin in June, 1948 in an abortive attempt to take the city. Berlin had been divided into four sectors of control. The Allies - the United States, Britain, and France. Each held one sector of the city collectively labeled as West Berlin. The Soviet Union held the fourth, East Berlin. All of the land area surrounding the city lay entirely in the Soviet zone of control. By denying the Allies access through their zone by road, the Soviets were able to block food and coal shipments to the Allied sectors of Berlin! It was an untenable situation that could have led to war!

To defend their interests, the response by the United States, Britain and France was to jointly establish a system to supply their sectors of Berlin by air. They created what became known as the "Berlin Airlift"." It was hard to know from one day to the next if hostilities were going to start between the Soviets and the Allies. What eventually became known as the "Cold War" had begun in full force! Despite Allied hopes for a quick resolution to the Soviet blockade, the Berlin Airlift continued until September, 1949. The more than 550,000 sorties were flown to Berlin brought in 500,000 tons of food and 1.5 million tons of coal, plus sundry other items, which even included seedlings to replace trees lost during World War II. It was a case where a stiff, united, Allied backbone fed the city of West Berlin and eventually forced the Soviets to back down.

The distance from Bremerhaven to Marburg was about 260 miles. The German countryside, while still war torn in places, was beautiful beyond belief. I enjoyed watching the scenery as the train slowly passed by. The railroad track on which the train traveled was called "narrow gauge" which was considerably narrower than track used in the United States. The small passenger cars were pulled by a midget steam locomotive which huffed and puffed its way slowly up the steep hills toward its destination. After what seemed an eternity we eventually arrived at Marburg, detrained and were taken by bus to a Replacement depot called Tannenberg Kaserne. Tannenburg Kaserne sat atop a large hill and consisted of various buildings as well as several large, well kept, stone barracks. It had been the home of German troops during the recent war. Now it was ours.

Shortly after arriving at the Replacement Depot at Tannenberg Kaserne, those of us who had been together since we boarded the General Maurice Rose at the Port of New York, began to be transferred for duty in other parts of Germany. I was there long enough to be able to go into Marburg on pass a couple of times and seem to recall the poor quality of the champagne and the exquisite beauty of the city's girls. But then I was a twenty one year old soldier and single. I have since learned that as we age our interests change.

After a couple of weeks at Marburg, my orders came through. I had been assigned to Headquarters and Headquarters Company, 7797 Signal Depot Group, in Hanau. The base was located about 2 miles east of Hanau on the Main River and about 20 miles east of the city of Frankfurt. In 1949, it was the only Signal Depot Group in the European Command. Its mission was to receive, store, issue, and provide 5th echelon maintenance for all signal equipment issued to the Army of Occupation forces of the European Command as well as equipment required to carry out additional missions charged to the Chief Signal Officer, EUCOM. It also operated signal field procurement teams to procure various types of signal equipment from the German economy and to rehabilitate equipment and items worth repairing.

My job turned out to be somewhat different than I expected. Here I was, a twenty one year old kid assigned to manage and oversee workers in the Depot's electric shop, most of whom were either Germans or Displaced Persons who had been taken (usually against their will) to Germany from their countries of origin to assist in the German war effort. They were working for the Occupation Forces while waiting to go home. Many were electrical engineers and highly skilled in various electrical fields. My only qualification was that I had been a maintenance electrician for Firestone Tire and Rubber

Company and had also worked for a couple of electrical contractors between the time I left the Navy and joined the Army. Surprisingly, we got along very well.

One of the German electrical engineers I became friends with was a man named Wilhelm Veal. He lived near the small town of Lagendiebach not far from the base, raised a couple of pigs and had a wife and family. Since my grandmother on my father's side had been born in Mecklenburg, Prussia, they kind of adopted me. I spent a lot of my off time at their home. "Willie's" wife made wonderful strudel and stuffed me with it. "Willie" (bless him) introduced me to homemade German salami, courtesy of his pigs. It was to die for! He also drove me into Frankfurt a couple of times perched in the sidecar of his BMW motorcycle. He kept me from sticking my foot in my mouth more than once in the electric shop and he did it in such a way that it made me look a lot more qualified than I was. I will never forget him or his wonderful family.

Things went along pretty well for a few months until one day I started having problems. When I woke up the air around me looked like it had big, clear, holes in it and my head was spinning. I had no idea what was wrong so I went on sick call. When I told the medic on duty my problem I guess he thought I had lost my mind. I ended up as a patient at the 97th Army General Hospital in Frankfurt. I have little recollection of how long I spent there or what was done for me. I vaguely recall that at some point I was transferred to an Army hospital, in Wiesbaden, and I do vividly remember one of the procedures I was subjected to while a patient there. It is one of the most unpleasant memories of my life. I never knew why it was given to me but I will never forget it. It was electro convulsive therapy or ECT.

The way electro convulsive therapy was administered by the Army in 1949 in Germany and how it is done now is as different as night from day. Today, much more effective and much safer methods are used in treating mental illness. Back then is was pure horror! I remember being led up a long hall to a small room that held a table with a thin mat on it. A young looking doctor told me to get up on the table and to lay down. No muscle relaxants of any kind were used prior to the "treatment"." A device bearing a set of electrodes was simply placed bilaterally on my temples, a plug was put in my mouth and bam, I had a full scale convulsion! Lights out! I would wake up sometime later aching all over, my memory affected, wondering what had happened to me.

Today's method of applying ECT for severe depression, as well as other indicated mental health issues, is far safer than it was back then. The introduction of succinylcholine, in 1951, allows for a brief duration of muscle relaxation during the treatment and, along with the use of a general anesthetic, prevents the bone shattering convulsions that I had to endure back in 1949. Modern medicine has arrived at the conclusion that ECT must be used very cautiously in people with epilepsy, or other neurological conditions, because, by its nature, it produces small tonic-clonic seizures. As years went by and medicine progressed, VA doctors eventually realized that I had temporal lobe epilepsy...probably due to my fall from the top of a triple decker bunk while serving in the Navy, at Great Lakes, in 1945. Kind of like having your own "built in" shock machine!

From the Army Hospital, in Wiesbaden, I was taken to Bremerhaven and put on a hospital ship, the USNS Comfort, to be sent to Walter Reed Army Hospital back in the States. I recall very little of the voyage, where we landed, how I got to Walter Reed, or how long I was there. Due to the electro convulsive therapy back in Wiesbaden, big chunks of both my short term and long term memories for that period of time had disappeared. Much of it is still missing after 65 years.

After my stay in Walter Reed, I was transferred to Brooke Army General Hospital in San Antonio, Texas. I had lots of time on my hands and I used some of it to pick up two years of college credits with help from the United States Armed Forces Institute. I was still a patient in Brooke General Hospital when the Korean War began on July, 1950. I was Honorably Discharged from the Army on August 14, 1950, with a 30 percent service-connected disability rating, and returned home to St. Petersburg, Florida. At the age of just 23, I had served in two different branches of the military, during two different wars, had been medically discharged from both, had received mustering out pay from both, and, despite a lot of practice on firing ranges, hadn't fired a single shot in anger at the enemy! I wondered what else the future held for me or if I really had a future? Time would tell!

I interrupted the mental retreat into my past for a moment and raised my single eye toward the Interstate, watching vacantly as it flowed rapidly by. I realized we were almost at the half way point to Trinka Davis Veterans Village Community Living Center and what was an unknown future for both Jeanne and myself. Tonight, she and our cat, Snoopy, would be sleeping in the small apartment in Emeritus Riverstone Assisted Living in Canton and I would be spending what was left of my life in what I regarded as a VA nursing home. Nice, but still a nursing home. If I could have peeked into the future I would have realized how wrong I was. Trinka Davis' amazing gift to the veterans she cared so much about would give me a reason for living!

I returned to reexamining the years gone by, picking up where I had left off. Returning to St. Petersburg hadn't supplied the satisfaction that I had hoped for. During the years I had been in the Army, many of my old friends had moved on with their lives. Although I enjoyed the opportunity to spend time with my parents, whom I loved dearly, it was time to get on with my life. So in early 1950, I packed up the 1929 Peerless I had bought for a hundred and fifty dollars and headed back to Akron, Ohio, where I had lived before joining the Navy. I will never forget that trip! Six flat tires on difficult drop center rims that had to be changed on the way. The hunt

30

for an electric fuel pump to replace the one that had given up the ghost. The trip took twice as long as expected. It was a nightmare!

When I finally arrived in Akron, I junked the old car and received the magnificent sum of thirty five dollars. My next move was to find a place to live so after a short search, I rented a room from a nice elderly lady. As my new digs were within walking distance of a Goodyear Tire and Rubber Company plant I applied for and got a job as a zone electrician. Although I had to work the late shift it paid well and life got a bit easier. It was then that I met the girl who lived next door. She worked as a waitress at the Cottage Lunch Restaurant where I ate most of my meals. After a short courtship we got married in July, 1951. I was 24 years old. She was just 18. After a few months in a small upstairs apartment, we were expecting our first child and decided we needed more space. We rented a lakefront home on a small, but beautiful, lake. I drove back and forth to work in an old car I had purchased. Life was pretty good until winter came. The snow fell; the temperature dropped below zero; the lake froze solid and so did my car's battery. Enough was enough! We packed up the old car and headed for Florida where it was warm!

After moving to St. Petersburg our first daughter was born in May, 1952. Work in the construction field had been slow and I needed to make a living to support a growing family. I took a job selling encyclopedias and on the day our first child was born made enough money to pay the entire hospital bill. Later, I worked for the U.S. Post Office, first as a clerk and later as a substitute carrier. My medical problems had followed me from the service and required numerous trips to VA doctors for treatment.

In 1953, I was hospitalized, at Bay Pines VA Hospital, for blackouts. Because I had a propensity to fall asleep without warning the doctor assumed I had narcolepsy. He prescribed a combination of dexedrine and diamox. Dexedrine, which is supposed to keep you awake, had the opposite effect on me. It put me to sleep! As for the Diamox, I read years later that it actually can reduce epileptic seizures. During the next ten years I took dexedrine and diamox and did not require any hospitalization. A doctor ahead of his time or just plain luck? I really do not know.

From the hospitalization in 1953, until 1963, the dexedrine/diamox combination enabled me to function with only minimal treatment from the VA. I became involved as a partner in two electrical contracting firms, in St. Petersburg. In 1957, I qualified as a Master Electrician, in Pinellas County Florida, one of the most populous counties in the state. Later, I worked for a major electrical contractor and supervised some large commercial jobs. Then, I became interested in politics. My first effort was to run for City Council, in St. Petersburg. I came in a respectable third place in a field of six candidates. In 1960, I ran for State Representative and won the Democratic Primary over the party's chosen candidate by a two to one margin.

In the General Election, I was the only Democratic candidate for office, in Pinellas County, who publicly supported John F. Kennedy. While Florida, in 1960, was a state controlled by Democrats, Pinellas was a heavily Republican County. Both John F. Kennedy and I lost the county by huge margins. John F. Kennedy became President and I became a legislative consultant who also ran political campaigns. I took to my new occupation like a duck to water! In 1962, I ran campaigns for the Democratic party's candidates, in Pasco County, Florida. All won their races in a landslide victory over their opponents.

Things were going great until late that year my problems accelerated to the point that I literally fell apart. I spent several months in Bay Pines VA Hospital. While I have little recollection of the whys and wherefores of what put me there, VA records reflect that I was given heavy medication and fifteen electric shock treatments. The medication caused serious side effects and did the opposite of the purpose it was given for. Big chunks of my memory simply disappeared and never returned. I was discharged from the hospital and my service-connected disability was raised from 30 percent to 100 percent permanent and total.

While I was in the hospital, my first wife found someone else and in 1964 we were divorced. She went her way and I went mine. Evidently my problems, caused by what had happened to me in the military, were more than she could handle. In retrospect, I can understand her actions and hope

33

she has had a happy and fulfilling life. My one regret is the effect it had on my three daughters.

Life went on and, in July, 1967, in a most unexpected way, I met my beautiful Jeanne who became the "love of my life"." I had remained active in politics and a friend of many years came to me with a problem. A good friend of his family's husband, a local businessman, was in prison having been convicted of running a gambling operation. As they had two small children she was desperate to have him home. She had gotten her minister and church congregation involved and they had started a petition to have him released. Because my friend was a good man, I agreed to look into the matter. In checking, I discovered he was a "first offender" who had never even had a traffic ticket. I agreed to do what I could to help. While I won't go into details, he quickly came up before the State Parole Board who decided to put him on parole. His wife was so overjoyed she came to me and asked how she could repay me. Not knowing what to say, I simply told her to find me a "nice girl" to date.

A few weeks later she called me. She informed me she had found a girl she thought would be perfect for me. It seemed Jeanne had come from Endicott, New York to visit her sister Eleanor in Pinellas Park, Florida, and Eleanor was her close friend. She had invited them both to dinner and wanted me to join them. Being single, and tired of eating in restaurants, I agreed. At least I would get a good "home cooked meal" out of it. I got that plus a lot more than I ever expected! Jeanne and I were married in Endicott, New York, October 7, 1967. It was a love match from the beginning and has remained so for the past 47 years.

In early 1968, a few months after Jeanne and I were married, I traveled to New York City by bus to check the Grand Lodge of New York's records searching for information about a York Rite Masonic sword I had been given by a friend of the family when my father died, in 1956. It had belonged to an officer assigned to the Constitution (Old Ironsides) who had served during the Civil War when it was used as a training ship. After a day's research, a snowstorm prevented my return to Endicott. I spent the night in the nearby YMCA. I had the desk clerk put the sword in the safe, intending to pick it up in the morning.

The next thing I remember was waking up in Washington, D.C. VA Hospital. It was several days later. I found myself in a hospital bed with tubes in both arms. I remembered nothing of what had happened or how I got there. Back in Endicott, my wife, who was deeply concerned, contacted the Police. They put out an APB to attempt to locate me. Five days later I was found at the Masonic Service Association office in Washington, D.C. by Chief Field Agent Bill Edmunds and Field Agent Danny Knode, who realized I was very ill and needed immediate medical attention. Going through my effects they found a Masonic Dues Card and a few papers in a briefcase indicating I was a disabled veteran. My wallet was missing. They contacted the VA Hospital and in an hour had me there. For the first few days I was on the critical list. The MSA contacted my wife Jeanne, who got on a bus and traveled twelve hours, in a snowstorm, to Washington, D.C. to be at my side. Chief Field Officer Edmunds, who was also a Methodist minister and his wife, Hazel, took Jeanne into their home treating her as a member of the family, while I was in the hospital.

The whole story of what happened made headlines on the front page of the June 1968 "Your Masonic Hospital Visitor", a publication of the Masonic Service Association of the United States and is distributed to every Masonic Lodge in the country. The headline, credited to my mother who lived in St. Petersburg, was based on her statement to Chief Field Officer Edmunds: "SURELY THE HAND OF GOD DIRECTED HIM"." I still have a copy of the publication and will never part with it as it demonstrates the true meaning of Brotherhood! The Masonic Service Association is a wonderful organization that maintains Field Offices in Military and Veteran's Hospitals. They offer their services to all active duty military and veterans in need regardless of whether they are Masons or not.

Prior to my trip to the Grand Lodge in New York City, Jeanne and I had been planning to relocate in St. Petersburg. When I was well enough, I was flown to Florida and reported to Bay Pines VA Hospital for further treatment and care. During my stay there, I received a "Grand Visitation" by Grand Officers, from the Grand Lodge of Florida. Between

Washington, D.C. and Bay Pines Veteran's Hospitals I spent a total of 40 days as a patient before being discharged.

As we rolled along the Interstate, I recalled major events in our lives since the day Jeanne and I were married. So long ago and so much had happened. First and most important was the adoption of Julie (10) and Craig (5). Jeanne's two youngest children by her first marriage. It gave me a son and another daughter who I had come to love as if they were my own. And with the approval of the judge they were! Julie grew up to be so much like me it is scary! She earned her Bachelor's Degree in Physical Education from the University of Central Florida. Craig had one year of college at Campbell University and after a difficult life filled with problems, passed away at 50 years of age.

My daughter Sandra by my first marriage, became a dietitian. She received her Master's Degree from the Florida State University. She wrote numerous, best-selling, books on healthy eating, served as President of the Florida Dietetic Association, in 2004, and made numerous television appearances, including one on the Oprah Winfrey show. My stepdaughter, Cheryl, earned a Master's Degree in Chemistry and had a very successful career. She was with Cornell University for a number of years and is currently with Wells College in Aurora, New York. All of my girls made me very proud of their accomplishments.

From 1968 through 1981, life for me became somewhat difficult. According to VA medical records, I became a patient

37

in VA hospitals twenty times. Medical problems during that time period included a seizure disorder, a stroke, a pulmonary embolism, several incidents of blood clots in my legs, atrial fibrillation, four rectal surgeries, three incidents of hepatitis, and "endogenous" depression. To complicate matters, I developed severe reactions, including stupors and comas, to the anticonvulsants and other powerful drugs prescribed to treat me. As one excellent internist, Dr. Stan Trigg of Blue Ridge, Georgia who treated me for 24 years, later wrote in a letter to another physician, "The most important thing to know about George is that he does not metabolize drugs the same as everybody else. It takes his body much longer to eliminate drugs than it should. This is hard to believe until you see it happen"." That was putting it mildly!

But life goes on. In between hospitalizations, I remained active. In 1969-70, I was President of St. Marks Eight, a salvage operation interested in salvaging sunken Spanish Galleons off the Caribbean coast of Colombia. With the help of friends in the Roman Catholic Church, I was able to obtain the first permit ever issued by the Colombian Government for that purpose. I was also named as a Director of the Kennedy Memorial Fund of Colombia, serving with several respected clerics and the wife of the country's former President. During the mid and late 1970's we spent two non-consecutive years in Black Mountain where I served as a Consultant to the Christian Action League of North Carolina and as Executive Director of Concerned Citizens of Asheville and Buncombe County, an organization of churches consisting of several different denominations. While in North Carolina, I was hospitalized twice in Asheville VA Hospital and once in the VA Hospital in Durham.

As Julie's car moved on toward our destination, my thoughts rolled back, to 1980, when we had moved to Eustis, Florida, and bought a home. My seizure disorder worsened and it caused me to go into a deep depression. I began treatment, at Gainesville VA Hospital with Neuropsychologist, Dr. Warren Rice and Neurologist, Dr. Wilder. After treating me for about a year, they decided to try me on a new drug. I was placed in the hospital under the care of Dr. Germine Odenheimer who put me on Tegretol. For me, it was like I had received a miracle! The seizures stopped. Although I continued to require outpatient care, I was able to stay out of VA hospitals for the next eleven years.

Stopping the seizures enabled me to function again. During our seven plus years in Eustis, I ran several political campaigns for candidates of both parties including a couple for my close friends, State Representative Everett Kelly and School Superintendent Carl Pettitt. I was also active in the election of Representative Buddy McKay, to Congress. Kelly later became Speaker Pro Tem, of the Florida House of Representatives, and Buddy McKay became Lt. Governor. He also served as Florida's Governor for a short time after Lawton Chiles passed away. I was deeply honored to serve for four years during the 1980's as a member of Congressman McKay's

39

Service Academy Selection Committee for Florida's Sixth Congressional District. Our assignment was to assist him in selecting nominees who would be awarded scholarships to the United States Service Academies.

During the 1980's, despite my service-connected disabilities, I was able to again become involved in veteran's affairs serving the DAV Dept. of Florida for several years as Deputy Legislative Officer and in 1983-84, as its State Resolutions Chairman. As a disabled veteran it was then, and is today, my major interest.

In February 1987 after back to back freezes practically destroyed Lake County's citrus trees, we decided to move from Eustis to the north Georgia mountains. Jeanne and I were basically small town folks and loved the closeness and rural atmosphere they provided. After some searching we found and purchased a large four bedroom brick ranch style home, near the Toccoa River, about two miles from McCaysville. The house came with an acre and a half of gently rolling land and sat high on a bank surrounded with pines, maples, oaks, and dogwoods. It overlooked a large green pasture that blended into "trout filled" Wolf Creek and the side of a small mountain beyond. It was "our little bit of paradise" and we planned on spending the rest of our lives there. We almost made it.

We blended easily into the community and for nearly a quarter of a century we got to know and love the mountain folks. Jeanne joined the Copperhill Iris Garden Club where she served as President and Secretary. She also did volunteer work for the Whitewater Olympics and on the tourist train that ran along the banks of the Toccoa River from Blue Ridge to McCaysville. We both joined the local AARP Chapter and were active in our church. In addition to going back to Florida every two years to run campaigns for my friend, State Representative Everett Kelly, I served a couple of years as Secretary for McCay Lodge No. 423, F. & A.M.; transferred my DAV membership to Chapter 28 in Blue Ridge and dabbled in local politics. I also served for two years in 1988-89 as a member of Ninth District Congressman Ed Jenkins Service Academy Selection Committee.

Although the Tegretol had stopped my seizures, I still required care for the residual problems that came with it, including bouts of depression and occasional spells of irritability. Since my home, near McCaysville, was 118 miles from the Atlanta VA Medical Center, I applied and was approved for VA Fee Basis care from local doctors. I made occasional trips to Atlanta VA Medical Center and things went along pretty well until it was discovered I had melanoma (cancer) in my left eye. My eye was removed in November 1992 at Atlanta VA Medical Center. After that I could no longer drive in Atlanta traffic. Being so far from the VA, and not wanting to depend solely on Fee Basis care, I purchased an AARP supplement for my Medicare. It was a good thing I did because VA Fee Basis for disabled veterans, in my area, became so poor, in 2008, that doctors were often not paid and many times phones at the Atlanta Fee Basis Office were not even answered. I needed an eye exam and my numerous requests were of no avail.

Finally, I had had enough! In 2009, I sent a couple of certified letters, to someone in Washington, D.C., explaining my problem and telling him how it affected veterans in my area. Soon after, the VA called me from Atlanta (four times in a single day) and approved my eye exam. In addition, I was provided with transportation from my home to Atlanta VA and given geriatric care at the Bronze Clinic. That was my lucky day! I was placed under the care of Dr. Rina Eisenstein and she continued to treat me for the next five years. She kept me alive.

My mind whirled in protest as I continued my review of the past. Suddenly as we approached Douglasville, a voice issued from the back seat of Julie's car. My grandson Cory, at an inch over six feet in height and about 225 pounds of solid muscle and an eating machine loudly announced he was hungry. We stopped at a Steak and Shake to get something to eat, then continued our journey toward Carrollton. We would be there in just minutes. The thought was depressing to me. It meant the end of my life with Jeanne with assisted living for her and a VA nursing home for me.

As we continued toward our destination, I recalled how idyllic life had been for us in the mountains over many years. Suddenly, things changed. Jeanne began to have memory problems and it became difficult for her to cook or drive. I had two serious falls requiring emergency treatment at the local hospital. Our daughter Julie, who had frequently been driving 70 miles to help us put her foot down and insisted we move to Canton so she could look after us. She picked out a two bedroom/two bath ground floor condo with a garage in Riverstone Villas and we bought it, sight unseen. It turned out to be ideal. Riverstone Villas is a small community of only 82 units mostly occupied by seniors. Tucked away from the hustle bustle of city life and surrounded by woods. It had a Clubhouse, pool, exercise room, and library. Stores and even a movie theater complex were nearby.

We packed up our treasures of twenty five years and downsized by giving a lot of our belongings to charity. We moved to Canton on December 3, 2011 and shortly thereafter sold our home in the mountains near McCaysville. Things went fairly well for a few months until on May 17, 2012 I fell down several steps at the Cherokee County Courthouse landing on my head and neck. Sheriff's Deputies called an ambulance and was taken to the local hospital. I was diagnosed with a "brain bleed" and transferred to the Neurosurgical section of Atlanta Northside Hospital. From then on it was all downhill!

In August, 2012, during a visit to Atlanta VA Medical Center, my blood pressure skyrocketed. I was hospitalized for five days, during which time an inferior vena cava filter was implanted to prevent blood clots in my legs from going into my lungs. I lost much of the use of my left arm and leg due to

43

spinal cord compression at C2-3 near the top of my neck. On May 9, 2013 I had a cervical fusion and it removed the pressure off my spinal cord. I regained some of the use back in my arm and leg but it was obvious time was running out for us. And today it had.

As Julie's car approached the gate at Trinka Davis Veterans Village Community Living Center, I turned off my mental recollections of what my life had been like during the past seventy years. It was replaced by a dark cloud of hopelessness as deep as anything I had ever experienced. Somehow I had to keep up appearances for my family. My last thought as we approached the entrance to the facility where I was to spend what little time remained to me, were two non-contiguous verses of a poem I had written in February, 2014, while deeply depressed. It reads like this:

SAGA OF A DISABLED WORLD WAR II VETERAN
By George Woodruff

Time has passed me by and now I'm sick and old, nearly blind, kidneys failing, stenosis crippling my spine.

A pair of painful legs that no longer function or up me hold, a power wheelchair for this worn out old carcass of mine.

So I guess I'll bear this continual depression and pain.

Until the Supreme Architect above finally takes me away, So God if you are somewhere up there listening to my prayer.

I will really appreciate it if you decide to do it today!

CHAPTER FOUR

The Miracle of Trinka Davis

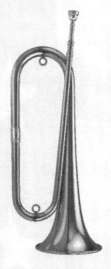

On May 15, 2014 shortly before noon, we arrived at the Trinka Davis Veterans Village Community Living Center. Julie looped her vehicle around the parking area and entered the curved driveway under the overhang that faces the stone walkway leading to the front entrance. My son-in-law Tom, had arrived minutes before us, his van "packed solid" with my belongings, including a power wheelchair and a 42 inch color television. He had parked in a space nearby. As Julie pushed the button that opens the back hatch of her Toyota Venza SUV and left the car to retrieve my large rolling walker. Tom exited his van. He began to walk toward us. My wife Jeanne and my grandson Cory, got out quickly to join them. I sat quietly in my seat for a moment before getting out, trying to push back the feeling of hopelessness that tormented my soul. I forced a smile as Julie helped me with my walker.

The five of us walked slowly down a wide, buff colored, stone pathway that led to a pair of wide double doors located at the front entrance to the facility. As we entered the building, a tall, muscular, uniformed Dept. of Veterans Affairs Police Officer came out of a small office on the left to inquire into our

46

purpose for being there. We were identifying ourselves to him when Jennifer Talley, the attractive young Clinical Social Worker that Jeanne, Julie, and I had met on our first trip to look over the facility a few weeks prior, came up to us and greeted us warmly. At her direction, we followed her down a hall and turned right to a section of the Community Living Center known as "C-House", further identified by its residents as "Liberty House"." We entered the "House" and proceeded to Suite C-109 which was to be my new home.

Julie, Tom, and Cory left to get my belongings out of the van. Jeanne and I remained behind wanting to spend our last bit of time together. I looked around and surveyed my new living quarters. The suite in which I expected to spend my remaining days consisted of a short hall with a sink, mirror, and metal clothes rack, a spacious bedroom, and a connecting, well designed, bathroom. One side of the bedroom sported an attractive wooden countertop, about two feet wide. It ran the entire length of the wall. Below the countertop, and built into it, were six large drawers, a pair of wide doors that concealed shelving and an open space that served as a desk. Above the countertop hung a small color television that had been fastened to the wall.

A huge set of windows covered the back wall and provided a sunlit view that overlooked a large, paved, turn circle and a parking area that graced the far end. The turn circle held an island in its very center that was somewhat unique. It was filled with small, leafy, trees, various shrubs, and yellow colored flowering plants that gave it a stunning look of life. The large bedroom proved to be all anyone in my condition could possibly need or expect. Superbly designed, it contained a big closet with sliding doors, an extra wide hospital bed that could be adjusted electrically to suit its occupant, a night stand and a comfortable recliner.

Near the bed was an adjustable table that, when needed, could swing a wide arm over the bed. Its purpose was to provide a method whereby a bedfast resident could be served meals and receive necessary medical treatment. In square footage, my new home was probably about as large as the small apartment Jeanne would be occupying at Emeritus Riverstone, in Canton this very evening. Its one major drawback was, that from this day forward, I would have to live without her by my side. Although our ages and infirmities had left us with no other choice but the one we were making, it was still an extremely difficult situation to be in.

While Tom, Julie, and Cory were making the several trips necessary to transport my belongings from their van to my new quarters, a number of staff members began to stream in to welcome me. They introduced themselves but there were so many I simply couldn't remember all their names. I do recall one elderly veteran who whipped his power wheelchair into my living area, introduced himself, handed me a letter of welcome and left as quickly as he came. Although I would eventually come to know everyone very well, and come to appreciate their competence and kindness, things happened so fast that my "first day reaction was one of pleasant bewilderment.

My "welcome" to Trinka Davis Veterans Village Community Living Center included being presented with a ringed Handbook with my name, my suite number and a slogan "YOUR HOME, OUR COMMUNITY" on the front cover. It contained a lot of information about the wonderful treatment I could expect while living here and what was expected of me in return. It sounded almost too good to be true! My first reaction was one of skepticism. "Promises, Promises", I said to myself. But as time passed, I would discover they really meant what they said!

Tom, Julie, and Cory carried in the last of my belongings and, with Jeanne's help, began to quickly put them away. My power wheelchair was parked snugly on the right side of the short hall under the metal clothes rack. My clothes were either hung in the closet or placed in the spacious drawers. My books and other incidentals were relegated to the shelves under the countertop and my toilet articles were placed in drawers under the bathroom sink. The only thing left was my 42 inch color television which sat on the floor. But not for long! Two large gentlemen in work clothes entered my suite. They walked directly to the small TV hanging on the wall, quickly removed it and replaced it with my much larger television.

All too soon, the time came for Julie, Tom, and Cory to return to Canton. They needed to avoid the afternoon's traffic jam on the crowded Interstates and help Jeanne and our cat, Snoopy, get settled in their new apartment at Emeritus Riverstone assisted living. I kissed Jeanne one last time as they departed and we hugged each of them tightly. I would miss my family terribly as we had always been very close. The dark feelings of depression I had been trying so hard to conceal returned in spades. With a mighty effort, I choked back the tears. This final move from our life together in our condo in Canton, to a "VA nursing home", where I would live out what remaining time I had left, sad and alone, was by far the most difficult thing I had ever been faced with. It was like a punch in the gut!

After my family left, I rearranged things to suit me. I had always been a "fussbudget" and besides it occupied my mind getting my thoughts off the joyless future I was facing. Time passed slowly but eventually a knock came on my door. A feminine voice called out, "Time for supper, Mr. Woodruff." I walked out my door and rolled my walker toward a table in the kitchen/dining room area. This would be my first meal in my new home. I had no idea what to expect. Depressed about no longer being able to take care of my wife and having to leave our home, I had paid little attention to the area outside my quarters when we first entered C-House. This time I checked it out.

The first thing I noticed when I raised my eye was that a large room had been divided into two sections separated down the middle by a half partition. The portion toward the front entrance contained a number of comfortable recliners and a huge television that hung on the front wall. The second half of the room contained a dining table and a kitchen area. The kitchen was not in use and had been walled off from view by construction material. I wondered what was going on. I moved toward the table. It was long and wide and had some kind of colored, plastic, tablecloth on it stretching its entire length. It appeared to be capable of seating about 15 people. Several of the chairs were already occupied by veterans of all ages and colors. Some of the chairs had been removed and pushed up against the back wall to make room for residents in wheelchairs.

I parked my walker against the unused kitchen wall and sat down to the right of the elderly veteran who had earlier zoomed into my suite in his power chair and handed me a letter of welcome. It turned out that his name was W. J., that he was a World War II Navy veteran and he was just a couple of months shy of ninety five years old. The grizzled old buzzard's body bore signs of his age and infirmities but a gleam of intelligence shown through his piercing blue eyes and his mind was sharp as a razor. On my right was L.B. He was an African American Army veteran who served during the Vietnam era and a caring man with deep faith in God. L.B. could always be counted on to do things for residents who were unable to help themselves. Directly across from me sat O.W., another World War II Navy veteran. O.W. was a decent man, the kind that can be depended on. He and I both had a

51

propensity for unexpectedly falling and he like me bore numerous scars from his accidental dives toward the floor. As time passed the four of us would become good friends.

As the days flew by I got to know other of my table mates. There was J.M., a tall, muscular, African American and an Army Vietnam War veteran, who walked with the aid of a cane. J.M. was a man whose kindness and integrity was obvious from his actions...the kind of man you would want for a friend. And then there was C.B., a World War II Army veteran who had been twice wounded in action and awarded Purple Hearts. C.B. was eighty eight years old and still able to walk with a cane. Hard of hearing, his neck was bent to the point it almost touched his shoulder. C.B. was "country" and the kind of man whose handshake was his bond.

The remaining residents of C-House included J.G, a retired Army Sergeant First Class, who was in a wheelchair, R.M., also wheelchair bound and badly disable and F.L., who walked carrying his oxygen tank strapped across his shoulder. In addition to his hobby of constructing model airplanes, he was retired Air Force and an excellent, self-taught, artist. The last resident was C.H. a thirty three year old veteran who seemed to have some kind of a neuromuscular problem. He was unable to talk and had to be fed through the stomach with a tube. He was quite intelligent and could read and point to letters on an alphabet board to make his desires known. I was to learn more about each man as time went by.

A couple of weeks had passed since my admission to

Trinka Davis Veterans Village Community Living Center. I was having a miserable time adjusting to my new surroundings. Living without my sweet wife of forty seven years by my side kept my feelings of depression going full blast. I tried my best to keep them from the staff and the other residents and confine them instead to the times I was alone in my suite with the door closed. It was a case of "grit your teeth and keep going. At times it seemed almost too much to bear.

Suddenly, one evening I started getting an unusual feeling that I can only think of as "the jitters"." My systolic blood pressure reading shot up to 220 and remained in that vicinity for a sustained period. Apparently, I was having what can be best described as a "hypertensive crisis"." A "hypertensive crisis" is a severe increase in systolic blood pressure where the reading exceeds 180. It requires "urgent care" because it can cause damage to your organs and lead to a stroke. And "urgent care" is what I got from the staff! And plenty of it!

The Registered Nurse who was on duty when my "crisis" happened contacted Dr. Jamya Pittman the young, attractive female physician who was in charge of medical care for the residents of the Community Living Center. Dr. Pittman, despite the fact that she was off duty at the time, came quickly, examined me thoroughly and prescribed a drug named clonidine, which works by slowing down your heart rate and relaxing blood vessels. She debated sending me to the local Emergency Room at nearby Tanner Hospital in

Carrollton. I told her I didn't want to go so she stayed right beside me until she was certain the drug had done its job.

The clonidine worked for a time but, as Dr. Pittman had warned me that the effect didn't last. My blood pressure rose again and I had a rough night. For a few hours I wondered if my residency at Trinka Davis Veterans Village was going to be a short one. Still depressed, I really didn't care much one way or the other. There seemed little purpose left in living. I had made my peace with God and had no fear of dying. That fear had disappeared back in February, 1995 when I had a cardiac arrest and "died" in the back of an ambulance on the way to Fannin Regional Hospital in Blue Ridge, GA. It was an experience I will never forget. I actually heard the Paramedic who was unable to get a blood pressure reading say to the EMT "Flat Line"." As I gently floated out of my body, I watched them as they worked to bring me back and I heard every word they said. It was the most peaceful feeling I have ever had; completely without fear and full of joy.

I awoke the next morning, my hypertensive crisis much improved, figuring God must have allowed me live for a purpose. As to what He could possibly expect from an 86 year old, 100 percent service disabled veteran whose main method of transportation was a power wheelchair was beyond my comprehension! But I had l earned over a very long life not to try to "second guess" Him. When I got out of bed I began to look around. It was as if I was seeing the purpose of Trinka Davis Veterans Village for the first time. And what I saw really opened my eyes! There was nothing even remotely like it in the whole VA system! The facility was nothing short of amazing! In that moment, I realized that the story of Trinka Davis Veterans Village Community Living Center and the outstanding care it provides for veterans who had become seriously disabled while serving their country and could no longer live at home, was a story that needed to be told.

Imagine (if you can) a "nursing home" that that furnishes a private room and bath for every resident. Add to that a mixture of the most caring and competent staff of Doctors; Nurse Practitioners; Nurses and Certified Nursing Assistants you could possibly imagine. Then try to picture in your mind a facility where seriously disabled veterans have access to an attached, well-equipped and well-staffed, VA Outpatient Clinic; an experienced Psychologist, who comes complete with a therapy dog; a more than capable Social Worker; a dedicated Chaplain to provide spiritual comfort for those who wish it; superb Physical and Occupational Therapists; a Housekeeping staff that keeps the place spotless; a Maintenance crew who will happily mount your various pictures and awards on the wall for you; and a trained supervisory team to keep such a facility operating properly, all under one roof.

Sound almost too good to be true? That isn't even the half of it! Scads of dedicated volunteers come to visit, often bringing the residents welcome fellowship and services. Their numbers include several American Legion Posts; the Amvets and numerous local organizations. The Legion Posts feed us until our bellies almost burst with delicious popcorn, candy, soft drinks, and, oh yes, they also conduct Bingo games with prizes for the winners. Other volunteer groups visit us often; bringing homemade cakes, ice cream, and other goodies that we have come to refer to as "soul food"." And every three weeks on Thursdays a lady barber named Jerri gives us free haircuts. But what we appreciate most is the fact that they all honestly care about us and that we haven't been just shoved in a corner somewhere and forgotten.

Trinka Davis Veterans Village also provides transportation by way of a large, fully equipped, wheelchair friendly, van so those residents needing wheelchairs, walkers, or canes to get around can occasionally get to stores like Wal-Mart and Kroger and shop for "necessary" items like toilet articles and "unnecessary" forbidden goodies. The van's driver operates the wheelchair lift and helps us park our wheelchairs in the proper spot so he can attach stays to keep them stable. The van also comes fully equipped with a couple of CNAs who watch over us like mother hens; keep us on the straight and narrow and help those who need it get into the store's electric carts so they can drive around the stores to shop.

The many wonderful benefits I have described in the several paragraphs above could not have come about except for the caring actions of Trinka Davis, who provided the millions of dollars in funding necessary to construct the Community Living Center and the attached VA Outpatient

Clinic out of her own pocket. Although Trinka passed away in 2006 and never lived to see her plans come to fruition, the members of the Trinka Davis Foundation she created carried out her desires to help the veterans she cared about so very much to the letter. To those of us who live here what she accomplished is nothing short of a miracle! And somehow, somewhere, up in heaven, I believe Trinka Davis watches over us with a smile!

After reflecting on the superb way in which the Community Living Center operated, I came to the inescapable conclusion that the story of how this "one of a kind" facility came to be, the way it brought real meaning to the difficult lives of seriously service disabled veterans, and the work that the caring team of professionals assigned here did, in taking such excellent care of the residents in their charge, was one that the citizens of our great nation needed to know.

I pondered over how, through what seemed an extraordinary set of events, I had been lucky enough to end up in a place that gave so much to me and expected so little in return. I was first informed of its existence by my psychologist, Dr. Regina Sherman at Atlanta VA Medical Center, who had never seen the facility. Next I talked with my VA Social Worker Mrs. Lerch, who told me more about Trinka Davis Veterans Village CLC, and realizing it might be a good fit for me and arranged for my first visit there to "look it over"." Next came Jennifer Talley, the attractive, kindly, Clinical Social Worker at Trinka Davis Veterans Village who gave my family and I our first tour of the place. Finally there was my Bronze Clinic Primary Care physician, Dr. Rina Eisenstein who when told that I was going to have to put my wife Jeanne in assisted living, looked me in the eye and said "George, you cannot live alone"." She picked up the phone and started the ball rolling for me to become a resident of the VA's Community Living Center in Carrollton, Georgia. A series of coincidences? Who knows? Sometimes, strange things just happen.

Having decided the heartwarming story of Trinka Davis Veterans Village was something that needed to be written, the next move was how in the world to get it done. Was I really capable of undertaking such a major project? After all, I was almost 87 years old with only one eye and nearly blind in it. Vision in my remaining eye was about 20/150 which doesn't leave you with very much. I could barely see. I also had severe spinal stenosis and neuropathy in both legs and while I could travel very short distances with my large rolling walker, my main method of getting around was my power wheel chair. Add to that diabetes and renal failure and writing a book about anything doesn't make much sense. I had already had a serious bout with a "hypertensive crisis" and there was no way of knowing if I would have enough time left to finish it.

On the plus side was the fact that I loved to write and had been doing it in one form or another most of my life. I had written a couple of books in the distant past. "Day of

Indignation, (1996), and: Miracle at St. Luke's, (2002). Both were religious fiction set in the north Georgia mountains near where I had lived for a quarter of a century. They were probably no "great shakes" as books go but the local folks seemed to like them and I thoroughly enjoyed writing them. I had never tried writing "non-fiction" but I had come to believe that what was happening at Trinka Davis Veterans Village, CLC, was something that could be important to the future of care for seriously service disabled war veterans. Especially for those coming back from Iraq and Afghanistan with lifelong injuries that deserve the best care our country can offer. I concluded I would at least try to give it a shot.

Now that I had decided to attempt to tell the story the next thing was to come up with a fitting title. I racked my brain for a week but nothing seemed to fit. I sat on my bed trying to play my harmonica with lots of flat notes and little talent. When I tried to play an "off key" version of "Taps" it suddenly dawned on me. Most of us living here in the Community Living Center, would not be going home again. Our next destination would probably be to a cemetery where "Taps" is often played during a veteran's Committal Service. "JUST BEFORE TAPS" seemed to describe our current living situation to a tee! I picked up my magnifying glass; sat down at my computer and, in my "one finger style of typing", hammered out the title.

I soon discovered that writing "non-fiction" requires a ton of research. I would need to obtain the names of the residents in C-House, where I lived, as well as the names of residents in other houses. As it applied to the residents I decided for privacy reasons, I would use their first and last initials only. I also decided it was not necessary to discuss their various disabilities in specific medical terms, but I would like to note that admission to VA Community Living Centers, in most all cases, requires a service connected disability rating of at least seventy percent. My next task was to attempt to obtain a reduced size floor plan of the Community Living Center and the attached Outpatient Clinic plus a Table of Organization showing the names and positions of all the people who worked here.

There was still another chore to accomplish but it was an important one. It concerned a small book "Trinka Davis: Southern by Choice" that I had been given when I first came to the Community Living Center. It told the touching story of Trinka Davis' life and how Trinka Davis Veterans Village came about. Realizing I might want to borrow a couple of quotes from the book to better explain how Trinka Davis' concern for veterans led to her generous gift, I wrote to Nancy C. Hughes, who heads the Trinka Davis Foundation, asking for permission. It was graciously granted with a request that I share a copy of the finished book with the Foundation and she wished me good luck. Praying that I haven't bitten off more than I am able to chew, I can probably use a lot of it! Time will tell. The days passed slowly. In June I fell twice. First in the bathroom and two weeks later in my bedroom. I got skinned up quite a bit and the second fall cost me a 50 mile trip by ambulance to the Emergency Room at Atlanta VA Medical Center. I wasn't the only one who was falling. I had stiff competition for the "Falling Championship" of C-House in the form of O.W. Although we were tied at two falls each, O.W. would have won hands down if CNA Juanita Kirk hadn't grabbed him on the way down to the floor, in the hall, and if his tablemate, J.M., with a well-timed move, hadn't prevented him from flopping between the dining room table and the wall that separates the dining area from the living room. O.M. had a change of medication and seems to be out of the running, at least for now. My problem with hypertension still hung on but had abated somewhat thanks to Dr. Pittman and Nurse Practitioners Ms. Hill and Mrs. Warner, who watched over me like I was a newborn baby. God Bless you ladies!

As for the book, I had been trying to write it with the help of a magnifying glass to be able to read what I had written. It turned out to be slow work and not an easy job! On July 1, 2014, the problem was solved thanks to Dr. Douglas Blackmon, a highly skilled eye surgeon at Atlanta VA Medical Center. The cataract surgery he performed on me changed my failing vision almost immediately. On August 5th, I had my final post-surgical appointment at the Eye Clinic. Dr. Blackmon did the examination. The results turned out to be nothing short of amazing! My age related macular degeneration was mild and the retinal scarring they had been so concerned about turned out to be minimal. But the real "miracle" was that my former 20/150 vision had improved to almost 20/20, with glasses. For me, writing "JUST BEFORE TAPS" had just become more doable! I thanked God and Dr. Blackmon, in that order.

Life at Trinka Davis Veterans Village was getting better for me every day. My depression was lifting and my daughter, Julie, brought my wife Jeanne here from Canton to visit me every couple of weeks. In addition, we talked by phone almost every day. Sometimes my son-in-law, Tom, and/or my grandson, Cory, he of the large frame and huge appetite, came along. On July 28, 2014, we celebrated my 87th birthday with lunch at Longhorn and cake and ice cream later in the facility's Social Room. It was a day early but who cared! We were together! Things we're starting to look up at last!

For the most part, day to day activities in the Community Living Center go along pretty well. We, the residents, function more or less like a "Band of Brothers" who have our military service and our service incurred disabilities in common. Similar to a close family, we look out for one another and, when necessary, we have each other's' backs. From Bingo to Wal-Mart trips we do most everything together. A major part of our "extended" family includes the entire staff of folks who work here in C-House. They do for us what we can no longer do for ourselves and they do it willingly.

The members of the staff in C-House work together as a team. They always seem willing to go the extra mile for us. An example of the kind of caring help that comes to mind is what happened wh

between my bedro

bleeding and I coul

but I am a pretty big

get me off the floor.

Joe Hosier, one of o

Storm war veteran)

up like I weighed al

and began to patch

"family" atmospher

at the thought of the gre

missed. Maybe next

Ann Wyatt, the RN

mid-thigh le

circulator

de

Another prime example of the type of quality care we receive here in C-House concerns a ritual of a sort that happens every morning without fail. Our suites are cleaned from top to bottom with hospital perfection! One of the housekeepers who works in C-House, Donald Cotton, is kind of special to us all. When Donald enters the room, with his big smile and friendly disposition, everybody gets a lift. He doesn't have a mean bone in his body and always has a kind word for everybody. In addition to raising our spirits, Donald really loves his job. He cleans and sterilizes everything! No germs survive on his watch. Another case of a treasured "family member" always looking out for us!

Today, August 7, 2014, was drawing to a close. I have been a resident of Trinka Davis Veterans Village, CLC, for almost three months now. Because my blood pressure was out of control I had not been able to make today's trip to the American Legion's luncheon in Mableton. My mouth watered at food and delicious deserts I had month? I punched my call button and N on duty, came in and helped me into my gth boots that connect to my sequential

A sequential circulator is a pneumatic compression ice that pumps air into the boots, releases it, and pumps it in again. I like to think of it as a leg squeezer. Its purpose is to reduce the edema (swelling) in your extremities. It runs for an hour and then shuts off automatically. R.M. and I are the only two residents in C-House who need to use them and they do their job pretty well. I use mine three times daily. A click of the timer indicates that my hour is up and it shuts off automatically. While I couldn't get the boots on without help I have learned how to remove them. I turned off the circulator's switch and unzipped them gratefully.

Dog tired, I lay down in my wide, surprisingly comfortable hospital type bed; put my head down on the pillows and thought of my wife and family living so far away. I missed them so much but there was no other choice available to us than the one Jeanne and I had made. Emeritus Riverstone assisted living in Canton for Jeanne and Snoopy, and the Community Living Center seventy miles away in Carrollton for me. I thanked Almighty God for giving me another day to work on the Trinka Davis story and asked Him to watch over my loved ones. I closed my eyes and finally went to sleep.

CHAPTER FIVE

Life at Trinka Davis

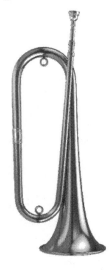

When you enter through the wide front entry doors of Trinka Davis Veterans Village Community Living Center you are in for a nice surprise. Your nose is not immediately blasted with that overwhelming odor of urine that dominates too many nursing homes and often seems strong enough too gag a maggot! Instead, you will be treated to the refreshing smell of "clean" that denotes a well-kept facility. No residents line the halls slumped over in wheelchairs for hours at a time, ignored and untended by the staff. Don't get me wrong. There are good, privately operated and well run, nursing homes that take acceptable care of their residents and they are probably in the majority. But I doubt if there is any nursing facility, private or VA, anywhere in this country that can hold a candle to ours. And it would not have existed to serve the needs of Georgia's service-disabled veterans except for the kindness and caring of Trinka Davis. God Bless her!

"C-House", where myself and other service disabled residents, reside is one of four separate "Houses" in the Community Living Center portion of Trinka Davis Veterans

65

Village. The "Houses" are designed to hold up to eleven residents. Each resident being provided with a comfortable private suite of their own. The "Houses" are further identified by being given the numbers "A", "B", "C", and "D"." As you enter one of these "Houses" through its wide double doors the first thing that catches your attention is the large lobby area filled with comfortable love seats and chairs. The front wall of the lobby area is lined with bookcases that are separated by the back side of a white brick chimney. When you step out of the lobby and enter the huge main room you can't help but be dazzled by the beautiful chandeliers that dangle from the high ceilings which are completely surrounded by wide glass windows. This added feature floods the room with glorious sunshine during the day and provides a stunning view of the moon and stars at night.

As you continue on, turn your eyes toward the middle and back of the main room. You will detect that it is split down the center by a horizontal half wall that separates the front sitting area from the dining area and fully equipped kitchen which actually merge into each other. The "sitting area" is furnished with comfortable recliners and a big, wall mounted, television hangs just above the wide white stone fireplace.

Well-appointed resident suites extend outward from the main room and on both the right and left sides. If you were to visit one of the residents in his suite you would generally find that he has festooned his long countertop and the wall above it, with loving family pictures and some of the numerous awards he has received at some point in his life. When residents first arrive, they are immediately encouraged by the staff to personalize their suites and give them as much of a feeling of "home" as is possible.   The fact that each resident has been given the privacy of his own quarters only adds to the "homelike" feeling. Actually, the Community Living Center, here at Trinka Davis, may well be the last "home" many of us ex-military residents will ever know. Precious "memories" of "what once was" tends to help make our lives here a lot easier.

One eye popping feature of the facility is a wide, open, field that extends the entire length of the VA Outpatient Clinic on one side and the entrances to all four "Houses", as well as the Fred Kelley Club House, on the other. Each entrance has a large covered porch protruding from it well furnished with wooden tables and chairs. The entire perimeter of the field area is encircled by a walkway wide enough to accommodate even the biggest wheelchair. Protruding from the outside wall, on the Clinic side, is a noisy waterfall that continually pours its contents into a walled pool below. The field itself has grassy areas on both ends that contain large flower beds. They are divided from each other by a fieldstone floor that contains more tables and chairs, some covered by large umbrellas to prevent the broiling rays of the sun from burning the occupants.

The fieldstone area is the site of regular barbeques,

often accompanied by bands and other top-notch entertainment provided by outside veteran and volunteer groups with assistance of the staff. The "menu" includes everything from ribs and chicken to hot dogs and hamburgers; all furnished with plenty of sides and deserts. One unusual feature that lines the sidewalk in front of "A" and "C" Houses is the multitude of pots belonging to residents. These "small pot farms" raise everything from tomatoes to okra. They are attended with loving care by their "farmer" owners and the mouthwatering produce they produce is occasionally shared with other lucky residents who are not so agriculturally inclined. Hint! Hint!

In order to show you why there is such a growing need for more facilities like Trinka Davis Veterans Village which provide comfortable accommodations, coupled with a high quality of care, for their seriously service disabled veteran residents, I will introduce you to a number of them. Each story is true and has been thoroughly checked for accuracy. To protect their privacy, I am using their first and last initials only. I have personally interviewed each one, where possible, and will pass on as much of their stories as I have been able to gather. Each has served our great nation with honor and distinction and each has paid a high price in the coin of lifelong disabilities that they received while serving in the military. All would do it over again in a "New York minute", if our country called, despite the price. Most, like myself, reside in "C-House" but a couple of the others I have written about reside in "A-House"."

Since you have already been beleaguered by my own personal "tale of woe", in Chapters One and Two, I will start with the story of W.J who, at 95, is our oldest World War II veteran and sometimes philosopher. W.J. and his wife were married in July, 1940, and had a son just a few months old. Had he wished, he could have easily been exempted from the Draft. Instead, W.J. a lifelong resident of West Georgia, volunteered to serve. Like many of his generation, he answered his country's call and joined the Navy, in July, 1942. He became a Petty Officer, rising to the rank of Storekeeper Second Class. He served on a number of different naval stations including Great Lakes, Norfolk, Port Hueneme, and Corona, California, Charleston, South Carolina, and Glynco Naval Air Station, home of the Navy's Blimp fleet, near Brunswick, Georgia, prior to becoming seriously ill, in 1945. After hospitalization, he was granted total disability and received an Honorable Discharge.

He returned home to Georgia and re-joined his wife and family. He looked for and found a job he was able to do. He was employed, first by a lumber company, and later by a plastic company. Both jobs required a lot of traveling. With the addition of a daughter, his family had grown larger. Eventually, he left the plastic company to start a lumber company which he owned and operated until his retirement. W.J. and his wife, received the coveted "The Book of Golden Deeds" Award for consistently serving their fellow man and for their kindness and compassion for others. Deeply spiritual and a strong family man, one of W.J.'s favorite axioms is: "If you can't love family you can't love God and vice versa"." In 1996, as their health began to fail, W.J. and his wife, went to live with their son and daughter-in-law. After more than sixty five years of marriage, his wife passed away in December, of 2005. Due to mounting health problems, W.J. went to live with his granddaughter, in West Palm Beach, Florida.

In 2013, W.J. became the first resident of "C-House"." He is an avid gardener, raising pots of tomatoes and okra which, after being subjected to a "guilt trip", consisting of hungry stares at his bounty, he willingly shares with the residents of "C-House"." Among his vices is the fact that he also maintains a bird feeder, which at first seemed to be completely ignored by the winged masses he hoped to draw and looked like it was a miserable failure. Suddenly, it was discovered by flocks of birds, small and large, and his bird seed requirements jumped from nothing at all to three or four feeder refills a day. W.J. also packs his quarters with a large variety of groceries, enough to stock a small convenience store. Among his virtues is the fact that he has been a member of the Masonic Lodge for more than 65 years and is an avid recruiter for American Legion Post 143, in Carrollton. I guess no one is perfect!

Writing a book, especially at 87 years of age, can sometimes be a bit harrowing! Things don't always go like you envisage. For example, I ran into an unexpected delay after finishing the story about the first resident and before starting my story about the second. Part of the delay was due to the amount of preparation required to write some of the other resident's stories. After interviewing several fellow veterans, I concluded that having them fill out a questionnaire that included their background information and then discussing it with them was easier than trying to rely on my memory and theirs. So far, it seems to be working out pretty well.

Yesterday, August 24, 2014, I was unable to work on "JUST BEFORE TAPS" due to an unforeseen episode of extremely high blood pressure accompanied by some mild chest pain. Unfortunately, I told "big" Joe Hosier, the LPN on duty. The first thing I knew the leads to an ECG machine were slapped on my hairy chest; a pair of nitroglycerin tablets were shoved under my tongue and an ambulance was called to haul my elderly carcass to nearby Tanner Hospital in Carrollton. I spent four and a half hours in the emergency room with a port in a vein above my right hand to allow quick access for life saving medicines or draw blood for testing.

When it was determined that I didn't have any real heart damage they sent me back to C-House in another ambulance. The EMTs wheeled me back to my room. It was only after I got through with my little episode that I discovered a complaint of chest pain means an automatic trip to the nearest ER., VA protocol requires it and frankly, it is a good idea. It might save your life! And now, back to the next story.

If you were to watch eighty eight year old C.B. as he hobbles out of his room toward the breakfast table on his cane; head bent to one side by arthritis; it might be hard for you to picture him as the same nineteen year old boy who sat bravely on a halftrack, behind a .50 caliber machine gun, firing steadily at attacking German troops in north Belgium. True, he can't hear you very well anymore so speak loudly if you talk to him. Being exposed to constant gunfire is hard on the hearing. But when you look into C.B.'s eyes you see the same steel and courage that, after being wounded in the leg by shrapnel fired by German artillery, sent him back into action where he fought until he was wounded again. This time he was sent back to the states. Awarded two Purple Hearts for his wounds and his courage, C.B. is an authentic hero!

And now on to the rest of his story. C.B. was born in Etowah, Tennessee, in December of 1925. He was drafted into the Army in June, 1943 at the age of eighteen. He started Basic Training at Camp Chaffee in Little Rock, Arkansas, but was unable to complete it because of a birth defect in his feet. He was then assigned to a work detail on base. From there, he was transferred to Company A, 48th Infantry Battalion, and sent to Europe. When the Germans moved into north Belgium, C.B. was selected to operate a .50 caliber machine gun while sitting in a revolving seat in a military halftrack that had been converted into a moving gun vehicle. This is a tough job and often with a very short lifespan.

After he returned to the states and was discharged, life

went on. C.B. married and fathered four children, two boys and two girls. He studied mortuary science and served his apprenticeship before taking and successfully passing Tennessee's exam for Embalmers and Funeral Directors. C.B. started his own Funeral Home in his hometown of Etowah where he served his community for many years. Time and increased problems from his war wounds eventually caught up with him and he could no longer live alone. Like the rest of us here, he ended up in C-House where he receives the care he has earned from a grateful government who appreciates his service and the price he paid for defending his country.

The next resident of C-House I want to introduce you to is F.L., a retired Master Sergeant and a seriously disabled veteran spent twenty years of his life serving our country in the U.S. Air Force. F.L. enlisted in 1949 and served during both the Korean and the Vietnam wars. He had a most confidential career as a Flight Engineer on a C-124 Globemaster that required him to hold a "top secret" clearance. For years, F.L. flew out of Warner Robins Air Force Base in Georgia; Kelly Air Force Base in Texas; and Hill Air Force Base in Utah carrying nuclear weapons to U.S. Air Force bases worldwide. The C-124 Globemaster is a huge airplane. Statistics list its wingspan of just over 174 feet; its length at 130 feet; its top airspeed at 320 miles per hour and its maximum load at 216,000 pounds. It was designed to carry heavy cargo including tanks, trucks, bulldozers, or up to 200 fully equipped soldiers.

F.L. flew frequently into Vietnam where he was exposed to both Agent Orange and occasional bullet holes in wings of his C-124 Globemaster. He was married and fathered two children, a boy and a girl. Like many men of Italian extraction, he has a big heart and occasionally, a short temper, especially when he believes things are not done properly due to someone's neglect. And maybe he has a point. After he retired from the Air Force F.L. had a deli business; did building maintenance for the U.S. Postal Service and crafted stained glass. Eventually his service connected disability caused his health to worsen to the point that he needed the type of care that is provided here at Trinka Davis Veterans Village, CLC.

F.L. is very talented. He paints extremely well and has recently finished a painting of a leopard's face that looks so real you think it might bite you. He also builds model airplanes that are a sight to see. Like C.B., F.L. paid a high price for his service to the nation he loves. He is well respected for his abilities by those of us in C-House!

Yesterday August 29, 2014, was J.G.'s 63rd Birthday. His wife brought him a beautifully decorated Birthday cake and a large, lip smacking tray of cupcakes which he, unable to withstand the soulful glances of his tablemates in C-House, offered to share. In honor of his generosity, however reluctant, his is the next story I will share with you. It is interesting and a bit unusual.

J.G. retired from the Army as a Sergeant First Class on

December 31, 1992 after serving for twenty two years. His military career began with advanced individual training at Fort Gordon Georgia's Southeastern Signal School. After he finished, he was sent to the Pentagon for a polygraph test and, after passing, he was assigned to the elite United States Army Special Security Group. The USASSG was a group of officers and enlisted men who provided military intelligence and telecommunications support to the Commanding General and Chief of Staff of various Army posts in the Continental United States as well as worldwide overseas Army commands.

The position J.G. was assigned was not an easy one. It required both a "top secret clearance with special codeword type accesses" and superior intelligence. This allowed him to receive and transmit Special Intelligence messages as well as "eyes only" correspondence to and from General Officers and State Department Officials as well as U.S. Embassy personnel. Messages were processed over teletype equipment, enciphered and deciphered over communications security (COMSEC) equipment. Additionally, J.G. was tasked with couriering message traffic and briefing General Officers and other high ranking officials.

J.G.'s job required him to spend many years of his career on overseas duty. He served in Korea during parts of 1971-72 and 1976-77; Germany in 1972-74, again in 1981-84 and yet again in 1989-91; 1974-76 found him in the Southeast Asian countries of Vietnam and Thailand and 1987-88 found him in the Middle Eastern country of Turkey. He met his lovely wife, of thirty seven years, during his second tour in Korea, in 1976-77. They were married in Oklahoma in December 1977. To say J.G. got around would be putting it mildly.

J.G. served the last two years prior to his retirement, during the period known as "Desert Storm" or the First Gulf War. He began to develop medical problems near the end of his career. After his retirement, he was unable to find a job in his career field so he retrained himself to be able to drive an eighteen wheeler hauling airline cargo to and from several southeastern region and mid-western states. In 1994, a couple of years after his retirement, he applied to the VA for service connected disability compensation. He was awarded forty percent. In 2005, as his condition grew much worse, it was increased to one hundred percent.

Starting in December 2013, J.G.'s health had failed to the point that the Veterans Administration placed him in a private nursing home in Lake City, Georgia. He was at that time, and still is, confined to a wheelchair. Accommodations there for someone in his condition could charitably be described as "arduous"." Privacy, such as we have here, at Trinka Davis Veterans Village CLC, was non-existent. He was assigned to share a room with another man. Their unvented bathroom connected with another two man room meaning four very sick people were forced to share a public bath and a single commode. In March, of 2014, he was relocated here, to C-House, and a decent life...the kind our military heroes deserve to live..."JUST BEFORE TAPS"."

Over the past months, I have come to know the subject of my next story pretty well. L.B sits on my right at mealtime, in C-House, and is what can best be described as a "hearty eater"." He is also my friend. L.B. is sixty five years old, medium tall, without an ounce of fat on his muscular African American frame. He is one of the finest men I have ever known and is quick to help those of us who cannot get around as well as he does. His memory has been affected somewhat by his service connected disability but the inherent decency that is an important part of who and what he is has remained unaffected.

L.B. enlisted in the Army in Greenwood, Mississippi, at the age of nineteen just as the Vietnam War began to heat up. He served his country with honor for seventeen years. Six of those years were in Germany and two more were in Korea near the dangerous DMZ (De-Militarized Zone). He was a radio operator and attained the rank of Staff Sergeant. He also developed high blood pressure while in service, and was honorably discharged in 1986. After leaving service he drove an eighteen wheeler truck for a while but the medical problems developed during his long years of service finally caught up with him in the form of two strokes and made it impossible for him to continue working. L.B. is a widower with two grown children, a boy and a girl, who visit him often. Sometimes it is a little hard for him to recall specific dates and places but he does it to the best of his ability. Unfortunately, a lot of L.B.'s "story" must remain locked in his mind. I wish I were able to tell it to you better because his modesty makes me believe it is little short of amazing. I do know L.B. paid a high price for his long and honorable service to his country. He has more than earned the very best care it can offer in return. Fortunately, Trinka Davis Veterans Village CLC, provides him with that kind of care!

J.M. is an African American and a modest man. He was drafted and served in the Army from 1966 to 1968. Over a year of his service was in Vietnam in combat areas where bullets were flying and survival was by the grace of God. It is my hope that his story will help the reader understand the price of war both during service and after and how it affects those who fight the battles.

J.M. is sixty seven years old. He was born in Meriwether County, Georgia, in the unincorporated community of Durand a few miles from the Little White House where President Franklin D. Roosevelt spent many summers basking in the healing waters of Warm Springs. Prior to entering the Army, J.M. worked for General Motors in the Truck Department on the assembly line. After he was inducted, he was sent to Fort Benning, Georgia, for training and then to Fort Belvoir, Virginia. He was assigned to Company 576, of the Third Ordinance Battalion and shipped to Vietnam. J.M. was assigned to the Motor Pool as a mechanic and as a Security Guard at a U.S. Army Ammunition Dump, in Long Binh. Now comes the sticky part.

In February 1967, Viet Cong raiders cut through a barbed wire perimeter fence at the 3000 acre Ammunition Dump, where J.M. was stationed and placed time charges amongst a stack of ammunition. When the charges detonated live shells were tossed into other stacks of ammunition and all hell broke loose! To escape the flying bomb fragments and continuous explosions he and others ran to sand bunkers where they were forced to stay for hours. That and other horrifying war related experiences during his year in Vietnam left J.M. with the kind of scars that time doesn't easily erase.

After J.M. was discharged he tried to return to his former job with General Motors but was unable to handle it like he had prior to being drafted. He later served as a substitute teacher, in Albany, Georgia and also as a CNA in a nursing home. Everywhere he went the memories of what had happened during those days of combat went with him. In 1997, the Veterans Administration rated him as one hundred percent service disabled. Eventually, he ended up in a private nursing home paid for by the VA near Fort McPherson, where he spent two long years sharing a room with another person. The room had a bathroom that was connected to another room so four people actually ended up sharing one toilet and a shower.

Heroes like J.M. who have laid their lives on the line for their country and require lifelong care for service connected disabilities as a result, have earned a decent place to spend living out what time they have left. That finally happened to J.M. when he was transferred to Trinka Davis Veterans Village. Here, in C-House, he enjoys a private room and bath, great care and the camaraderie of other disabled veterans who can relate to his condition. I only wish there were more patriotic individuals of means, like Trinka Davis. Her thoughtful gift honors those seriously disabled veterans who unselfishly served our country in time of war and paid a very high price for their service. She, and the Foundation she created, have made it possible for some of us to live out our lives with respect and with relative comfort.

The last three stories about the disabled veterans who live in C-House concern R.M, C.H., and O.W. They are not as complete as the others but they are every bit as compelling. Two of the men are in their eighties and have been able to live as full of a life as their service injuries would permit. Not perfect but at least the sort of life that brought them the periods of happiness and sorrow that come to most of us. The third, C.H., is in his early thirties. Because of what happened to him in the military, he has been deprived of the life experiences most of us take for granted. When you read his story shed a tear and say a prayer for him and his family.

R.M. is a quiet man in his late eighties. He is severely disabled and requires a lot of quality nursing care. Where he served, what he did, and how he became disabled during his time in service is somewhat of a mystery. His ability to recall events may not be quite what it was in days long gone by. He doesn't want to talk about his service very much, even to the other veterans in C-House. By doing a lot of digging, I was able to learn that he served in the Army for twenty five years and retired as a Master Sergeant. He is of African American heritage with a very light complexion, and is pushed to the dining table for his meals by one of the CNAs because he is unable to make it on his own. His medical problems are serious and complex. They include diabetes for which he is given daily shots of insulin. His period of service began at the end of World War II and extended through both the Korean and Vietnam Wars. He is married and his lovely wife comes to visit him often. Their affection for each other is obvious.

C.H. is a thirty three year old Army veteran who served in Iraq during the Iraq war. He cannot tell you his story personally because his service connected disability has taken away his capacity to verbalize anything much beyond some sort of a grunting sound. He cannot eat in a normal fashion and has to be fed by the staff through a tube in his stomach. Whatever happened to him when he was in the service also brought about some sort of neuromuscular disorder that has rendered him unable to use his hands in a normal fashion. In order to communicate his needs to others with the small letter board that he carries he must hold one hand tightly over the other hand and, with great effort, force a finger to point to a single letter at a time.

C.H. has a wife and a child who visit him often. He is very intelligent and from the way he interacts with his family, capable of great love. Of all the disabled veterans who live in

81

"C-House" his is the greatest loss. And yet he bears it without complaint. C.H.'s condition is irreversible and the price he has paid for his service entitles him to the finest care the nation that he served so well can provide. Because there exists a Trinka Davis Veterans Village Community Living Center he is able to have it. As I said before, please shed a tear and say a prayer for him and his family. His is the high cost of war!

O.W. will be eighty seven years of age in November, 2014. He is a one hundred percent service connected disabled veteran from Walton County, Georgia, who served in the U.S. Navy during the latter part of World War II. He was discharged in 1947 after being a patient in Corona Naval Hospital, in Norco, California. Due to his health problems, the story he tells seems to change frequently making it hard to verify. O.W. states he served on LSD 22, the Fort Marion. From his description of the ship it is obvious that he did at some point in time.

The Fort Marion (LSD 22) was launched on May 22, 1945 and commissioned on January 29, 1946. It was a Dock Landing Ship of the Casa Grande class. It arrived at San Diego, its home port, on May 26, 1946, and through the next three years repaired landing craft, carried cargo and landing craft between San Diego and San Francisco while taking part in amphibious training exercise. While there is no record that it saw any action during World War II, it did serve with distinction during the Korean War and received several commendations.

O.W. uses a walker to get around and falls frequently. He and I appear to be engaged in a falling contest of some sort that neither of us really wants to win. During the four months I have lived in "C-House" he has fallen twice and I have fallen three times. Since he is quite frail and I am well-padded the damage to us both seems about equal. O.W. is a friendly man who often seems to be somewhat confused. Trinka Davis Veterans Village CLC provides him with the kind of care he needs and deserves. His disability is patently obvious and it was received at some point during World War II. I wish I could get the complete story of what happened to him but that is no longer possible. I think it might be a humdinger! Unfortunately, time has taken its toll and O.W. can no longer tell it exactly as it was. Sometimes we have to be satisfied with the part we can get.

The next stories concern two of the disabled veterans who live in "A-House"." The first, H.Y., is a highly decorated former World War II veteran who spent eighteen months as a prisoner of war in Germany. The second, P.A., is a twenty nine year old veteran of the Iraq/Afghanistan Wars whose service incurred disabilities will probably require him to have nursing home care for the rest of his life. Because of his youth, his is by far one of the most touching stories.

H.Y. was born in Roopville, Georgia on March 11, 1923. He is a decorated World War II veteran who holds numerous Awards for his outstanding service including the Distinguished Flying Cross, the Meritorious Service Medal, the Air Medal, two Purple Hearts, and the Good Conduct Medal, plus several other decorations. His military service to our country began when he entered the U.S. Army Air Force, in 1942, at the age of nineteen. H.Y. attained the rank of Staff Sergeant while serving with the 376th Bomber Group which was part of the 514th Squadron. He flew numerous combat missions as a ball turret gunner on a B-24 Liberator bomber and was shot down over Italy on December 28, 1943 during his twenty seventh mission. During World War II the average lifespan of a ball turret gunner was said to be approximately three missions.

H.Y. was wounded when his plane was shot down and he was forced to make a parachute jump to survive. Upon landing safely on the ground, he was spotted and captured by German soldiers. He was taken from Italy to Austria where he spent a difficult eighteen months in Stalag 17 as a prisoner of war. He says sometimes he was treated fairly decently and sometimes he was tortured. During his period of captivity his weight dropped from 160 pounds to 115 pounds. He was liberated three days after the war with Germany ended. He was medically discharged and was rated at one hundred percent for his disabilities received in service to his country.

Upon his return to Roopville, H.Y. took up farming because he wanted the peace and quiet to deal with the terrible memories of what had happened to him during his twenty seven missions as a ball turret gunner and his unforgettable experiences in Stalag 17, as a prisoner of war. Eventually, caught up by his service incurred injuries and the ravages of age he could no longer live alone. H.Y. has been a resident of "A-House", since early 2013, and is receiving the care he deserves from the very competent staff at Trinka Davis Veterans Village. H.Y. is another of our true resident heroes who have paid a high price for defending our country during time of war.

P.A. is an African American service disabled Army veteran of the Iraq War who celebrated his twenty ninth birthday at Trinka Davis Veterans Village on September 23, 2014. He was born in Ozark, Alabama, and served in the military from 2008 to 2010. P.A. has been a resident of this facility for more than a year and will probably need to spend the rest of his life here due to his need for continuing care.

While serving in Iraq, during the war, P.A. contracted an airborne virus that went through his nose and into his brain doing tremendous irreversible damage. Despite several brain surgeries, he has serious short term, as well as some long term, memory problems making it impossible for him to function in a normal manner and have the opportunity to enjoy life as a successful, contributing, member of society. For P.A., it is a terrible and irreplaceable loss! The best our grateful nation can do for him is to give him top notch medical care and the finest quality of life possible for the time he has left. He has certainly earned it!

P.A. is a "gentle giant" of a man who, because of the way his brain now functions, has gained 140 pounds since his medical disability discharge. He eats constantly because his brain is no longer able to tell him when he has had enough. The ravages of his Iraq contracted virus and his many brain surgeries have left him somewhat like a person who has had a pre-frontal lobotomy. In many ways, P.A. is almost childlike. His is one of the most heart rending cases among the residents and to realize the price he has paid in serving his country leaves a lump in your throat. While P.A. will never be able to succeed on the outside he is receiving loving care from a concerned medical staff and enjoys the privacy and the feeling of having a home which he receives at Trinka Davis Veterans Village CLC.

Including my own story, I have only been able to write the stories of twelve of the twenty six service-connected, seriously disabled, residents who currently occupy "A", "B", and "C" Houses. In my humble opinion, these twelve represent a fairly good cross section of the type of veterans who reside here, the disabilities they face daily, and the kind of care required to provide them with a life that is worth living for the time they have left. Like the twelve I have written about, the other thirteen residents all have at least a seventy percent service-connected disability and all received their injuries during war time service. I wish I had the strength and energy left to tell the stories of what each one in our facility did during military service, and in their civilian life afterward, but this is just a little bit more than this worn out, eighty seven year old 100 percent service disabled veteran, can undertake.

*As to the number of vacancies remaining, at the time of this writing, at our Community Living Center, "B" House still has six while "D" House is completely empty. "D" House is being reserved for "special" residents, with memory problems and awaits the hiring of necessary staff who can provide the type of "specialized care" those future residents who will occupy "D" House are going to need.

And now on to Chapter Five and the surprising story of what life is really like for the service disabled residents in Trinka Davis Veterans Village Community Living Center!

CHAPTER SIX

Living as a Disabled Veteran

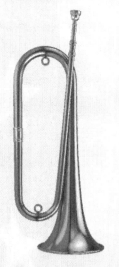

Did you ever stop to consider what it would be like if you became so badly injured from serving your country in the military, that you had to spend the rest of your life in a nursing home away from the family and friends that you love and who give your life meaning? Do you really think you could handle it if you were no longer able to get around by yourself except by using a wheeled walker or a wheelchair? How would you like it if you had to depend solely on the actions of underpaid employees to prepare your every meal; clean your dirty room; make your messy bed and provide the kind of daily care that makes your day to day life bearable? How would you feel if you had no privacy and were forced to share a single bedroom with another person you did not know? And what if you and that person were forced to share a single toilet and shower that was connected to the room next door that held two more people? Sound like the kind of lifestyle you would want for your remaining days? Of course not! But that is what is happening too many seriously service disabled veterans...right now!

What I described above is exactly the kind of sordid

living conditions some of our severely service disabled veterans (including C-House residents J.M., O.W., and J.G.) had to tolerate before transferred here to Trinka Davis Veterans Village CLC and sadly, there are still too many of our severely service disabled war veterans living in intolerable conditions like those aforementioned. Why is that? The answer is quite simple. There is simply nowhere else for the VA to send them! Facilities like this one built by the Trinka Davis Foundation with some seventeen million dollars of private money, donated by Trinka Davis and given to the Veterans Administration simply do not exist. It is one of a kind! It is my hope that patriotic people of means and organizations who care about decent living conditions for service disabled veterans, who have paid a high price to ensure America's freedom, act quickly to ensure it does not long remain so!

What is it that makes life here at Trinka Davis Veterans Village, CLC so different from life in other facilities that provide care for seriously disabled war veterans? Is it the decent living conditions? Is it the high quality of the care we receive from a staff that treats us like we still count for something? Is it the many dedicated volunteer groups from the outside who visit frequently to let us know that we have not been forgotten? It is all of these things and oh so much more! It is kind of hard to explain but it is somewhat like living in a "second home" where the people around you become almost like members of your family. Residents, regardless of ethnicity or skin color are kind of like "a band of brothers" with their military service and disabilities forming a common bond. The staff, some of whom are ex-military themselves, become like an extended family who look out for their disabled brothers and see that their needs are met with caring, kindness, and now and then a bit of humor.

To demonstrate what life here is like at Trinka Davis Veterans Village from day to day, I will try to explain it to the best of my ability based on my own experiences. For me, the morning usually starts with one of the staff knocking at the door of my suite at about 6:30 am. Like some others who live here in C-House I am, along with other serious health problems, a diabetic. In my particular case a blood sugar reading and other vital signs, must be taken twice daily. The process to determine my blood sugar begins by a staff member cleaning off the selected finger with an alcohol pad and zapping it with a small, spring loaded instrument that fires a sharp needle into the chosen digit with the speed of lightning. A drop of blood is then extracted by a hand held machine which beeps several times until finally giving the reading.

This particular morning, after banging loudly on my door to wake me up, it was long time CNA Morris Flowers who did the dirty deed. I could almost swear he had a sly grin on his face because I jumped a bit when the needle hit. Morris is a really great guy and a Desert Storm service disabled Marine. I served in both the Navy and the Army during a couple of long ago wars. Sometimes I wonder if Morris occasionally enjoys his work a little bit too much? Or it may be just another case of demonstrating to me the long standing rivalry between those who served in the Corps and those who didn't. Oh those Marines!

When my assaulted finger stops bleeding, I wheel my rolling walker into my large bathroom to perform my morning ablutions; slowly get dressed and then park the walker and climb onto my power wheelchair for the short trip to the breakfast table. When I arrive I generally discover that the early birds, L.B. and O.W., have gotten there before me, again. About the time I get my chariot parked under the table, ninety five year old W.J. wheels up next to me (on my blind side). He is usually closely followed by J.M., with his walking cane, R.M., in his wheelchair, F.L., with his shoulder carried oxygen tank, and C.B. hobbling out shortly thereafter. The rest of the C-House residents generally arrive in no particular order or sometimes not at all. Despite some occasional grumbling, mostly by F.L., the breakfast menu covers a wide range of selections and, depending on who is cooking, is usually pretty good. For the uninformed, grumbling is a "time honored" military tradition.

After enjoying a leisurely breakfast, we all go our separate ways as our schedules or personal desires dictate. I generally get on my computer to read the news; check political races and polls; read my e-mails and make appropriate replies. When I am finished I press the buzzer for help in putting on my zippered inflatable/deflatable thigh length boots that operate from an air pump. It has an hour timer so I sit back in my recliner and watch TV, sleep, or read while it squeezes away. If I any have "free time" afterward I use it to work on my latest book, "JUST BEFORE TAPS", for an hour or two. The "boots" are a three times daily thing which is a pain in the backside time wise but it helps keep down the swelling in my legs and feet.

Writing "JUST BEFORE TAPS" has turned out to be somewhat more of a task than even I expected when I first decided to do it. During my first five months at Trinka Davis Veterans Village CLC, I had a couple of severe bouts of hypertensive crises (high blood pressure), three falls to a very hard floor, problems with diabetes and a mini-stroke. This resulted in four bumpy ambulance trips to two different emergency rooms and quite a bit of lost writing time.

On the plus side, I also had eye surgery on my right eye, at Atlanta VAMC which restored my vision from 20/150 to 20/30 allowing me to continue writing. This was a big improvement for me as my left eye was made by the Veterans Administration. I keep hoping they will find a way to develop a vision chip that can be built into it. No luck so far but who knows what the future holds with the amazing advances in prosthetics. I also celebrated my eighty seventh birthday with my family present and lots of forbidden cake and ice cream.

There are so many interesting things for residents to do here that it is hard to list them all. Included among those numerous activities are frequent shopping trips to stores like

Wal-Mart and Kroger on a large VA van type bus. The bus has been specially designed so it can accommodate about a dozen disabled veterans, including up to five in "locked down" wheelchairs, plus a couple of CNAs and a driver. The CNAs come along to assist those residents who are so disabled they cannot shop without help and to deal with rare medical emergencies should they occur.

Unloading the Trinka Davis Veterans Village CLC, residents at one of the stores is a real "hoot"! Everybody is impatient to get going. They wait anxiously while the CNAs and the driver, who are stuck with the job of rounding up enough of the battery operated electric carts to accommodate those who need them so they can shop which is about everybody on the bus. When they finally round them up, they drive them back to the anxious, waiting, residents, and help them get into the electric carts. It looks like a game of "dodgem" as the disabled residents blast off like rockets headed for their chosen destinations which is usually the "goodie section" first. I think if someone posted the "event" on You Tube or Face book it would get a million hits!

As for the other available "by bus" activities, one of the favorites is the occasional trips to places that serve food. This includes restaurants like Cracker Barrel in nearby Douglasville and Longhorn Steakhouse, in Carrollton. Both are cases of "you have to pay for what you eat" and both are well attended by residents looking to get away from the facility's mundane daily fare for something special. Then there are those "free feeds" put on monthly by American Legion Post 264, in Mableton and Post 143 in Carrollton. The first is a buffet lunch with loads of food choices and the latter is a dinner served before the monthly Legion meetings. Post 143 also puts on a Saturday morning "country breakfast" which is held once a month in a church fellowship hall and includes my favorite "biscuits and sausage gravy"."

Other available activities offered during an average month, right here at Veterans Village, CLC, include frequent Bingo games put on by American Legion Posts 143 and 264 and the Amvets. All furnish popcorn, soft drinks, candy, and give prizes and/or small sums of money to lucky winners. As you have probably guessed they are extremely well attended. Water Aerobics is available weekdays for a small sum. The local Senior Center's facilities are also available to residents of Veterans Village for twenty five dollars per year and they offer many activities for attendees. There are several other "in facility" and "out of facility" activities to pick and choose from leaving little time for boredom.

All in all the Recreational Program for residents of Trinka Davis Veterans Village CLC is hard to beat due, for the most part to careful planning by two experienced, college educated, African American Recreational Therapists, Steven Duvalt and Anthony Beard. They are in constant contact with outside groups and organizations and, in addition to their many other duties, arrange for community outings that include trips to places like the Botanical Gardens and Day

Camps at Sweetwater Park. Another popular pastime for residents is going to bowling alleys, and semi-weekly fishing trips to a nearby lake. The champion fisherman in C-House is J.M. by a country mile. He seldom comes back with less than fifteen to twenty pounds of catfish which he cleans for cooking by the Chef. J.M. is also an expert at some kind of exercise dancing called Hip Hop ABS. I happened on the thing in progress one day while wheeling by in my power chair and almost split a gut laughing as he (and a bunch of others) were shaking their booties in time with the music. This you gotta see to believe!

Worship services are also on the calendar but not quite as frequently as I would like. The Chaplain, Reverend Monique Jimmerson, a tall, attractive, light skinned, young African American lady is currently "part time"." She holds "well attended" services in our small Chapel every other Tuesday. I will never forget one particular service that took place just prior to the surgery on my right eye. I was deeply concerned as the VA Eye Clinic's outlook for success wasn't too hopeful. Failure meant I could not continue writing this book without using a magnifying glass and maybe not at all. Since I had no left eye and the remaining vision in my right eye was a paltry 20/150 I asked those present to pray for success with surgery. Evidently their prayers (and mine) were answered as I came out of surgery with nearly perfect vision. Was it an "answer to prayer" or was it just plain luck? You decide. As for me, I prefer to believe it was the former!

To give you an example of how well the staff at Trinka Davis Veterans Village works with groups on the outside let me tell you what was done for me to help me solve a problem that at first seemed unsolvable. I am a Master Mason and became eligible for my sixty years of service Award on June 22, 2014. It was very important to me and I was looking forward to receiving it. But how? Being some 150 miles away from my home Lodge in McCaysville, Georgia getting the Award seemed nearly impossible. My power wheelchair only has a range of nine miles at four and a half miles per hour so that was out. To further complicate the situation, I cannot travel any distance very well, due to severe physical disabilities. I needed to be able to receive it right here at Trinka Davis Veterans Village or I might not be able to get it at all. I wondered to myself, "could something like this be done in a Veterans Administration facility?" I simply did not know and I had been almost afraid to ask.

After writing letters to various individuals attempting to solve the problem, without success, I was getting desperate. I finally decided to write to Georgia Grand Master, Edgar A. Land, who was head of all Masons in Georgia, and inform him of my dilemma. A couple of days later he called me on the phone in my room and informed me that my Sixty year Award would be presented to me by Buck Creek Masonic Lodge No. 639 and District 4 District Deputy Grand Master David Sullivan. I was excited with the good news and my excitement grew when Recreational Therapist Steven Duvalt came to my room and told me the time and date of the presentation. How he knew about it I still do not know but I am sure he had his finger in the pie somewhere along the line.

On September 23, 2014 at three pm, the presentation took place in the Fred Kelley Clubhouse right after the completion of the American Legion Post 143's Bingo game. As promised, a number of Brother Masons from Buck Creek Masonic Lodge, in Carrollton were on hand to assist DDGM David Sullivan with the ceremony. My wife Jeanne, our daughter, Julie, her husband Tom Shannon and our grandson Cory, had driven down from Canton, Georgia to be on hand for the grand occasion. Photographs were taken of the event and an article written, by Rickey Stilley, of the Times-Georgian. It appeared in the following day's paper. Boasting a bit? You are darn right I am! It made my day!

On every third Thursday, at exactly three P.M., a small miracle takes place here that brings great joy to the residents. An angel, named "Jerri", unfailingly glides through the front door of C-House. As she floats toward one of the empty back offices the residents from all over Trinka Davis Veterans Village, CLC, line up to follow her. They take their places in the hall outside and wait patiently for their turn to get a haircut. Since there is no barber at the facility, and most of us cannot get out to get our hair cut, the service she performs is beyond price! Jerri Williams is a dedicated "volunteer" who has owned the nearby Hairitage Styling Salon, since 1982. She cuts the hair of from fifteen to twenty veterans each time she visits no matter how long it takes. And she does it absolutely free! Refuses to take a cent and would be insulted if you offered to pay her. She says helping disabled veterans who have given so much is her way of "giving something back".." Her husband is a Vietnam veteran. Bless you for what you do so unselfishly, Jerri! You really are our angel!

Birthday parties are an important event at Trinka Davis Veterans Village! They come with ice cream, cake, and other delightful sweets that are dear to the heart of residents. The staff here puts on at least one per month and the Patriot Guard Riders of Georgia usually put on another. They are usually held in the Fred Kelley Clubhouse and are heavily attended by nearly everybody. It doesn't matter if any of the residents have a "real" birthday that particular month or not. We would sing "Happy Birthday" to a squirrel to get at the loaded goodie table. I'll admit the ice cream is sometimes "sugar free" but even that tastes pretty good. My personal preference is regular butter pecan! You bring it - We will come! In droves.

Another important event for me that took place here at the CLC was the celebration of our forty seventh wedding anniversary. It also fell on Jeanne's eighty fourth birthday. Our daughters Julie, and Cheryl brought her down from Emeritus Riverstone Assisted Living in Canton, so we could spend those precious few hours together. As to the "why" of the "double event" on the same day...it was my idea back in 1967 for us get married on her birthday. I thought maybe I could get by with giving her a single gift instead of two. Stupid me! Never happened. I also had the incorrect idea that I was the boss of our household. It took me twenty years to realize I wasn't. Women are smart. They have a way of making you think you run things when you really don't. They somehow twist you around their little finger and you end up doing what they want and believing it was all your idea from the start. And you love it! And her! With all my heart! Having Jeanne for my wife, all these many years, and Julie, Sandi and Cheryl for my daughters makes me four times blessed!

One thing all the residents of Trinka Davis Veterans Village look forward to is visits from family. Despite the private suites we live in and the excellent medical care we receive from the staff, this is still a life lived away from your loved ones. We are here because we are no longer able to take care of ourselves. Most, like me, get frequent visits from family members and it helps to ease the pain of separation. A few of the others are not so fortunate. They either have no families or families that, for some reason, seem to have forgotten they exist. A good, solid, recreational and volunteer program, coupled with a caring medical staff, helps a great deal to erase some of the loneliness in their lives and provides the feeling of "belonging" that is so important to all of us. And that is what Trinka Davis Veterans Village offers its residents....in spades!

It is mid-October here at Trinka Davis Veterans Village as I write this, and there is a slight tinge of color beginning to appear on the leaves of some of the nearby trees. It isn't the depth of color I remember seeing when we lived in the north Georgia mountains, near McCaysville, but there is enough to let you know there is a distinct change of seasons. Ninety Five year old W.J.'s tomato/okra pot garden has hung it up until next spring and the visits by the great feathered masses that populated his bird feeders all summer have abated somewhat. Southward migration I guess. There are still the large turtle doves that eat like hogs with wings and they perch on the feeder to stuff themselves instead of their former habit of eating the seed droppings left by other birds. Old W.J. takes it all with his usual accepting attitude, content to wait for the return of spring where the cycle is bound to repeat itself. F.L. continues with his models and paintings but I have noticed that, as of late, his propensity for griping has somewhat diminished.

As you walk toward the front double doors, of C-House you can spot L.B. his backside parked in a chair in front of the large TV, in the main living area, head nodding slowly as he fights off the urge to nap. O.W. and I look out for each other food wise. He loves cornflakes, which are frequently unavailable, and when I spot some I put them away for him so he can have them for breakfast. In turn, when the fruit is wheeled in and placed on the table in the dining room he grabs two or three choice bananas and saves them for me. We are both ex-Navy and we sort of look out for each other's interests. C.B., who has the suite next to mine, sits comfortably in his recliner making me wonder if he is day dreaming about times long gone by. J.G. still gets up late but is walking more...thanks to the help of Victor Ubani, RN, MSN, who is in charge of Restorative Care. J.M., who is the most active of the crowd, attends a lot of activities and appears to get a charge out of it. He remains his helpful self and is always on hand to meet the needs of others less agile than he. Like I said before, a real "band of brothers"."

A few weeks ago an event took place her that would have made You Tube if it wasn't so serious and problematical in nature. I call it "Kristin The Ant Killer"! Kristin Franklin is an African American disabled veteran with a seventy percent service connected disability and a Purple Heart for wounds she received in Iraq. She is also the housekeeper in charge of C-House and one very determined lady! As summer changed into fall, we discovered our digs had suddenly been invaded by hordes of sugar ants. They were everywhere! Everybody's suite, including mine, was loaded with the little buggers. The facility had supposedly been pre-treated, inside and out, by an exterminating company but, if it was, it sure didn't do the job. At all! The ant's invasion continued unabated and they finally discovered and saturated the kitchen garbage cans. Food and warm winter quarters. What more could they ask for? The ants must have sensed victory. I could almost visualize them thumbing their tiny noses at us in triumph. Silly ants. They had no idea of what they were in for!

Kristin's dander was up! How dare those little critters invade C-House? This was her domain! The war was on! She rounded up numerous spray cans of ant killer and the battle began in earnest. Spray cans in hand, she went at it suite by suite. If you could have seen the determined look on her face you would have been glad she wasn't after your hide. She even went outside the facility and sprayed the ground along the walls. It helped reduce the population considerably but the ants were not through yet. They seemed determined to try to hold on to their ill-gotten gains. Apparently, the food supply and the warm winter quarters were worth fighting for.

Finally, Kristin had had enough! She e-mailed Atlanta VAMC, explaining the problem and demanding help. Eventually, they sent one man to the rescue. It was enough! He brought bags of powdered ant killer with him and loaded the outside of the facility up against the walls with it. He brought baits into the suites and placed them where the ants couldn't miss them. They evidently mistook the baits for food and carried them back to their nests. Bad idea! If there were any ants left alive after the war was over they must have departed for elsewhere. Evidently concluding that Kristin Franklin, the Ant Killer, was way more than they could handle. We were glad to see them go.

Life here has its moments and it can be depressing at times. When you let your mind wander back in time recalling what was and then let it return to the present, facing what is, you can get that empty feeling in the pit of your gut. While "yesterdays" had their ups and downs you had so much living left to do and so much to look forward to. Suddenly (or so it seems) your time is about to run out and you are facing the uncertainty of leaving it all behind. You cannot know for sure exactly what lies beyond the grave because no one you knew has ever returned to tell you. But then something will happen to snap you back into reality and you realize that life goes on. My "snap" came this morning as I went out to eat breakfast and it made me realize that life is a cycle that is unending.

On Saturdays, most of the C-House residents tend to get a little extra sack time. I am not so lucky. My blood sugar gets drawn every morning about 6:30 am and getting punched in a finger with a needle makes any more sleep next to impossible. I exited my suite at about 6:45 am; poured my coffee and wheeled over to my place at the breakfast table. I realized I was the only one there which turned out to be a streak of luck. It enabled me to watch the interaction between three young ladies: Tamika Miller, our Chef; Heather and Toya both CNAs. Each one is a different stage in her life. It made me realize that life is never ending and it goes on from stage to stage and generation to generation.

The first Tamika is a young, attractive, happily married, lady with three small children. The second Heather and her soulmate are wildly in love and she has just entered the second trimester of her first pregnancy. The third Toya, glows with adoration for her fiancé. They are having pre-marital counseling sessions at their church by their pastor in preparation for their wedding. Tamika has enjoyed the ups and downs of marriage and motherhood; Heather is about to find out and Toya is preparing herself for the same kind of life experiences that Heather, in part, and Tamika, in whole, have already gone through. Each is in slightly different places in the cycle of life which constantly repeats itself over and over as generations pass us by. It snapped me out of my depression and made me accept the fact that life goes on, regardless.

Living here in Trinka Davis Veterans Village is anything but dull. The scale of events runs the gamut from pathos to humor. We live from day to day waiting for the advent of the grim reaper who eventually visits us all. We also enjoy a good laugh now and then, even if the joke is on ourselves! We have learned that life is what you make it!

CHAPTER SEVEN

The Good, Bad & Alarming

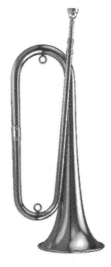

At Trinka Davis Veterans Village Community Living Center there are days that open with a bang and days that open with a thud. Today was a "thud" day. Just before five thirty am I was awakened by CNA Morris Flowers who informed me that the fire alarm was going off and it was time for me to abandon ship. I hadn't heard the noisy thing as my hearing aids were out for the night and I hadn't seen the flashing light because I was sound asleep. I managed to get my bathrobe and socks on, climb into my power chair and head for the rear exit.

All eleven residents of C-House lined up and poured out the rear door into the parking area accompanied by the staff. Wheel chairs and walkers filled with shivering, half-dressed men were herded or helped by staff members into a handicapped parking space to await the coming of the fire truck. It was a very cool morning and you could feel the mist in the air as it penetrated your bones. Residents of "A" and "B" Houses were nearby in other handicapped parking spaces to be out of the way of the fire truck. You could see the sleep in their eyes as they too shook with the cold. We waited impatiently for the sound of the siren. It never came. Finally, it was over. Thanks to a caring, well-trained staff, the fire drill was accomplished in record time. I hope it isn't snowing when the next one comes!

Sometimes, an apparent injustice (intentional or not) is done that really hurts a person by denying him a small privilege he has enjoyed for nearly as long as he has been a resident of this facility. It can change that person overnight from a kind, caring, old man who has reached out to help those around him; to a bitter individual who no longer sees the good in anything or anybody. It can even shorten his life. Such an unintentional injustice happened to W.J, a ninety five year old World War II veteran. Something he loved doing was suddenly taken away from him. You can see the hurt in his eyes.

W.J.'s wife passed on some years back and he was devastated. Their marriage had been long and loving and the loss was hard for him to deal with. Eventually, he came to live at Trinka Davis Veterans Village and found pleasure in raising tomatoes and okra in pots and installing feeders for the birds so he could view them from the window of his bedroom. W.J. was able to fill those feeders by using his wheelchair to go out a fire door near his suite. It was close to the feeders but it took great effort for him to even go that short distance. He loved watching the birds feed and it was one of the few pleasures he had left in his life. Suddenly, the tiny bit of pleasure he enjoyed so much was taken away by an act that, so far, seems to make little sense!

For some inexplicable reason, the VA evidently has concluded it is absolutely necessary to stop people from using that fire door.   No reasonable explanation has been given. The door has never had an alarm on it that could have sounded and caused a melee. W.J. has been using that door ever since he was permitted to install his feeders just outside his suite. Now, according to what he tells me, he is suddenly being blocked from access to his birds for no apparent reason. I wonder if whoever was responsible would have cared if they had known the only other way left for the old fellow to get to his feeders was simply too far for him to travel. Or was it just a case that VA regulations must come first and if they hurt an old man in the process, so be it? A lot of questions need answering. It would be a real act of kindness if someone could help W.J. find a way around this problem. It might give an old man who has done so much for so many a little bit of happiness for the time he has left. Or is that too much to ask? I hope not! Time will tell!

Today for lunch I had a Cobb salad. I didn't know what it was when I marked it on my meal form but, being born in Indiana, I figured it might have something to do with corn. It didn't. Actually it was pretty tasty especially when I added a few of W.J.'s olives and some of the blue cheese dressing I bought at Wal-Mart. As for the food served here it runs from very good to lousy depending on your taste!

As for me, I am a fussy eater. I do not like poultry. It reminds me of something that happened in the Navy in 1945 when I was stationed at the U.S. Naval Equipment Depot in Albany, California. I was walking by a large building on the base when my nostrils were assaulted by an awful odor. It was so overwhelming that I investigated. What I discovered when I looked in the window were rows of thawing chicken drumsticks plainly stamped with the year 1943. I can still envision those stinky, aged, thawing chickens every time it is on our C-House menu. Apparently, I am the only member of my family so affected. My wife and my daughters have eaten enough of the birds to stretch from New York to California. Ugh!

As for the daily menu, served here at Trinka Davis Veterans Village, CLC, it could use a bit of improvement. Currently, it is a "one size fits all" regular diet and, for some reason, it completely fails to take into consideration the need for special diets for residents with specific medical problems. Like several other residents, in C-House as well as the other two Houses, I am a diabetic. I can usually try to figure out some way around it to exclude the foods that raise my blood sugar level. I guess that is because my daughter Sandy is a dietician and has trained me pretty well. Others are not so lucky and eat everything on their plates. It is my hope that the "one size fits all" practice can be conformed a bit in the not too distant future to better serve the needs of residents. Enough of my squawking and back to the next item on my agenda which is lunch. I wonder what glorious culinary delights will be presented to us to tickle our palates.

Surprise! Surprise! Lunch was actually pretty good! A thick cheeseburger with all the trimmings; corn that actually didn't taste like our usual field corn similar to the sort usually fed to the hogs and an overabundance of tasty Cole slaw. Topped off with a diet coke! Will wonders never cease! Not exactly a diabetic diet but then a guy deserves a treat now and then. I will make up for my dietary wrong doing tomorrow or maybe the day after. Depends. Maybe dinner will be disappointing and I will have something to complain about. If not, I am sure F.L. will do it for me. He can always be counted on to find a flaw in something. Oh, those loud, hot-tempered Italians!

Dinner was a flop! Whoever came up with the idea of "vegetable lasagna" needs to go back to the drawing board. Anybody with a lick of sense knows that "lasagna" requires good cheese and a tomato based sauce combined with the appropriate pasta. The only other item on the menu was poultry so I ate a large bowl of "Special K" topped off with some bagged popcorn I bought at Dollar General the last time my daughter Julie was up for a visit. Not the greatest meal ever but it sure beats "vegetable lasagna" by a country mile.

I have the distinct hope that our "food problem" may be solved shortly due to an infusion of additional Chefs so that each House will be staffed for all meals. This might help in correcting some of the food quality matters that currently exist. At least it could eliminate the "cold food" problem that too often happens as food is brought from one House to

109

another without the use of a steam cart. We are very fortunate to have Dr. Kwanda McLemore, an excellent and thoughtful dietician, who understands the need for special diets for residents with specific medical problems. She is pushing hard to see that it happens as soon as possible. Knowing Kwanda and her concern for the welfare of the residents, I believe she may be successful.

One thing that makes Trinka Davis Veterans Village so special is that when problems arise the leadership here usually does its best to try to correct them. Sometimes this can be quite difficult. Final decisions are often made at the Atlanta VA Medical Center in Decatur, GA., fifty miles away from where the actual problems exist by folks who cannot be expected to completely comprehend them. It would be a step forward if this facility was given a little more autonomy to be able to solve the problems where they happen and where they are clearly understood by those who experience them. Wishful thinking? I sure hope not!

While most of the problems that exist at Trinka Davis Veterans Village are really inconsequential and few in number compared to the wonderful benefits it provides for seriously disabled war veterans, the one that bothers me most is the door to the laundry room. Those of us who are able wash our own clothes as it helps with retaining that feeling of independence that is very hard to let go of. The door in question is a very heavy fire door that can spring upon you without warning when you try to go in or out with your laundry basket full of clothes. Both O.W. and myself have been whacked four times by it leaving our arms bruised and bloody. No, we are not in a contest to see who gets banged up the most. But trying to get it fixed seems next to impossible. We will bring it up again at the next Resident Council Meeting and hope for the best.

Now that I have gotten the problems of our sometimes whacky, sometimes hilarious little world off my chest, I will close the door to the complaint department, for now, and get on with the story of what everyday CLC living is like from the viewpoint of an old curmudgeon (me) who has already lived several years beyond his allotted span. While I wish desperately I were still able to live at home with my wife the truth is I simply cannot. Old age and infirmity has caught up with us both so each of us has to settle for "second best"." In Jeanne's case, "second best" is a small assisted living apartment consisting of a bedroom, a small living room, a large bathroom with a shower and the ability to keep our crazy cat, Snoopy. She enjoys great meals plus a multitude of enjoyable activities and a lot of people similarly situated to become friends with. Not like home but not too shabby either.

As for me, I have a "second home" in Trinka Davis Veterans Village, CLC, as previously described with a lot of worn out disabled veterans who face the same kind of problems I do. When we are not engaged in Bingo or some other activity, we sit around and tell slightly embellished stories to each other while complaining about this or that.

Although we grouse a bit each of us knows that Trinka Davis Veterans Village is both completely unique and the very best the VA has to offer anywhere for the long term care of seriously service disabled veterans. However, we, the residents, reserve our right to complain loudly about flaws even though they may be only minor in nature. It is the military way of demonstrating satisfaction, but not too much. Two things you learn in the service, no matter how good things are, always complain a little and never volunteer. It keeps the command structure on their toes.

Today is a "feast" day. No, it's not some kind of religious holiday. It is the day of the monthly luncheon put on by American Legion Post 264 in Mableton, Georgia. The big wheelchair van leaves the facility here at about 10:30 am as the drive is fairly long. It is a day that few residents miss because it is a feed to end all feeds! Tables are loaded with food of all descriptions and you can eat until your belly busts if you are of a mind to. Unfortunately for me it is a meal I am going to miss. Woe is me!

I am having a mild problem with taking deep breaths, chest tightening and sudden weight gain so the shift RN "Me Me" (aka Jamilah Middlebrooks) called the Nurse Practitioner, Mrs. Warner, who rode to the rescue. After checking me over she ordered a chest X-ray, blood work, and, pending on the outcome, a possible increase in my dose of Lasix. Probably just some mild congestive failure which it not too unusual for an old goat like me. Keeping us old veterans perking along is kind of like working on a worn out vehicle that has long ago outlived its normal lifespan but they do their very best to try to keep us going just a little bit longer.

Today just got a lot more interesting if "interesting" is the correct word for it. "Me Me" came to see me with Bridget Thomas, the RN from one of the other houses, in tow. She had a blood drawing kit in her hand and a look of determination on her face. According to "Me Me", Bridget was the blood drawing expert but I really believe "Me Me" is soft hearted and just chickened out on the job. It took Bridget two tries but she finally got what she was after, smiled, and left.   "Me Me" then had me mount my power wheelchair and together we went to the X-ray department, in the Outpatient Clinic. While she found somebody to gossip with I was instructed to remove my shirt, grab onto a steel bar to keep from falling on my butt and put my chest flat against the upright X-ray board. Gosh it was cold! I almost jumped out of my skin!

After the ordeal was over we returned to C-House. It was "haircut day" and Jerri, the lady barber, was due to float in at three pm. I wanted to get as near the front of the line as I could so I shot past the nurse's office full bore and into the room used for haircuts. I saw thirty three year old C.H. (who I wrote about in a previous chapter) shuffling along behind me, trying to hold his hands still, followed by F.L. and J.G. We let C.H. go first so we could engage in a short bull session. Watching Jerri cut C.H.'s hair was something to behold and we looked on with interest. He wanted to be skinned on the sides with the top short but flat. C.H. is unable to talk so he makes his needs and wants known in different ways. Despite the fact that he is seriously disabled he got his point across well enough for Jerri to get it exactly as he wanted it. Looked pretty good too!

I was next in line and, as I don't have much to cut, it didn't take Jerri long. She did the best she could which turned out to be pretty good considering what she had to work with. J.G. has a full head of hair but F.L. tries to comb a few hairs over his big bald spot unsuccessfully. He doesn't fool anybody at all and probably not even himself! Bald is bald! Come to think of it that applies to me too! Every day here something new happens. Today it was the advent of a group of third year nursing students from the University of West Georgia in Carrollton. They were here to assess the resident's various medical problems or at least I think that was the purpose. A couple of them came into my suite to look me over. One pulled out a stethoscope, unbuttoned my shirt and slapped it on my chest while the other one observed. She also checked my eyes and missed the fact that the left one is prosthetic. This is a little joke I often pull on new doctors and nurses because the eye looks so good it appears to be real. When I told the student who missed it both began to look at my eye commenting on how real it seemed to be. I reluctantly relented and admitted I had pulled this little trick on a lot of folks and they had made the same mistake. I even caught an optometrist once.

They finally left my suite only to return several more

times. First they made my bed which may sound like a simple task but it really isn't. It is a three quarter bed and the VA (for some unknown reason) insists on buying full size sheets which do not fit the smaller mattress. To remedy this problem it is necessary for the bed maker to tie knots in all four corners so the bottom sheet will stay tight on the mattress. Fortunately for the students, who were going out of their gourds trying to figure what to do, CNA Juanita Kirk was on hand to show them. I'll admit they did a pretty good job after a few tries. I guess there is hope for them after all. Later, one came back to ask me my pain level. I realize they have to learn somehow and I guess practicing their chosen profession on me is something I will just have to put up with. Who knows? They might be working at Trinka Davis Veterans Village, CLC, one of these days. Maybe I had better smile and make nice instead of being a cranky old man!

Lunch time was approaching and I faced it with my usual apprehension. It actually turned out a little better than I expected which wasn't much. A toasted corn beef and cheese sandwich and some kind of soup that may have been broccoli or even mashed pea. It was hard to tell. Mystery soup might have been a good name for it. I put some salt in it to try to improve the taste followed by some "Mean Jean Hot Sauce" that came from Merceirs Orchard in Blue Ridge, Georgia near where we used to live in the north Georgia mountains. I was able to get half of it down but finally gave up. If "Mean Jean" won't fix it then it is a lost cause. A t least the sandwich was

115

pretty good. Thank God for small favors!

About three pm we had another fire drill. This time I was ready for it and was fully dressed. I grabbed a jacket, jumped in my power chair and it was off to the races. I was the first one to reach the back door entrance followed closely by J.G., in his manual wheelchair, which was being pushed rapidly down the hall by L.B. one of those rare individuals who always springs to help those less ambulatory than he is. At meal times he will get up out of his chair at the table to help C.B. who is in his late eighties and, with much difficulty, walks slowly with a cane. L.B. is a decent, caring man. I'll bet he was terrific as a soldier because of his bearing and attitude toward others. His is the "stuff" heroes are made of! Even after two serious strokes you can still see it in his deeds.

Today, Veteran's Day is being celebrated at Carroll County Veteran's Memorial Park in Carrollton, GA. The park was constructed to honor veterans who live in Carroll County and is a prime example of the deep feelings of patriotism that permeates this part of Georgia. While the celebration is being held three days early it is a day when most folks are off work and can, if they wish, attend the festivities. Special invitations have been extended to all World War II veterans who live at Trinka Davis Veterans Village. Most are going and will be loading on the big VA wheelchair bus to make the short trip. Regretfully, although I am a World War II veteran, I will have to miss this glorious occasion. I have developed a problem with increased fluid retention causing Dr. Pittman to double today's dosage of Lasix. Lasix is a drug whose purpose is to remove excess fluid from your system via your plumbing. Not conducive to extended periods away from accessible bathrooms. Maybe next year?

I am still having problems with fluid retention and my blood pressure is up so Lisa Leonhardt, the shift RN on duty, called Dr. Pittman who ordered another "double shot" of Lasix and a trip outdoors in the sun for some extra Vitamin D. She is an exceptionally thorough nurse and good at her job. I have learned that she and her husband have a penchant for Hershey's dark chocolate so I always lay in a supply of the little bars when shopping. After living in this facility for six months, the staff has become like a "second family"." They look out for us and we like to do little favors for them now and then to show them how much we appreciate them. I am not quite sure of how much dark chocolate gets home to Lisa's husband. From the way so talks about him it is obvious he is the apple of her eye so he probably ends up with at least half.

This coming Tuesday is a day I am really looking forward to! My wife Jeanne and our daughter Julie, are coming here to visit me on the "actual" Veteran's Day which is, as always, November eleventh. Julie brings Jeanne here from her assisted living facility, in Canton, every two or three weeks. We always go out for lunch at one of the local eateries. Veteran's Day some of this area's restaurants and businesses offer special "perks" to active duty military or veterans who can show proper identification. Among those proffering mouthwatering "freebies" are Longhorn, with free Texas Tonions and soft drinks and Olive Garden with a free meal from a special menu. Dollar General is giving veterans ten percent off on the whole purchase. As for the choice of restaurants, the selection will probably be made by my wife (or I will hear about it later) and I will load up with needed toilet articles and goodies at Dollar General plus a bag or two of treats for Snoopy, Jeanne's "live in" cat buddy.

With the start of another week it is back to "Restorative Care" which I sometimes reluctantly undergo five days a week. The purpose of "Restorative Care" at Trinka Davis Veterans Village, CLC, is to help keep seriously service disabled veteran residents, like myself, functioning at the highest optimal functional level possible while attempting to minimize our physical decline for as long as possible. If my inadequate description sounds like a "tongue twister" that is because it is. The program at our facility is headed by Victor Ubani, MSN-RN who came to the United States from Nigeria many years ago after finishing high school. Blessed with a strong work ethic, Victor buckled down, became an American citizen, got his four year RN Degree from American Sentinel College, went on to obtain his Master's Degree in Nursing, and is currently working on his Doctorate in Business Administration. He is a living example of what you can do if you are determined to get ahead and put your mind to it. He is also a very nice person.

Currently, my "Restorative Care" program consists of walking as far as I am able with my large, four wheeled walker.

Since I usually rely on my power wheelchair to get around, this is difficult, somewhat painful, but absolutely necessary if I am to maintain any degree of mobility. I have a considerable amount of weakness affecting my left arm and leg which exacerbates my problem. Victor, or his assistant, walk along beside me to make sure I don't fall and that I don't overdo. Walking is very important to me as I go out to lunch with my family members when they come to visit and their vehicles are not equipped to haul my power chair. This means I must be able to walk short distances with my rolling walker ergo "Restorative Care"." In addition, I lift small weights to try to strengthen my arms. Old age isn't for sissies!

Tuesday finally rolled around and Veterans Day was here at last! Veterans Day used to be called "Armistice Day"." Its original purpose was to celebrate the end of World War One and the date of the signing of the "peace treaty" in 1918 between the Allies and the Germans at Compiegne, in France. World War One was hosted as the "War To End All Wars" but it wasn't. As a result, "Armistice Day", in the USA, was changed to "All Veterans Day", (later shortened to "Veterans Day") sometime just before or during World War II. Other countries have different names for it. It is a good thing it was changed as there apparently is no such thing as a "War To End All Wars" and unless there is a major change in the makeup of human nature, I doubt if there ever will be. Our country has been involved in six major wars and several minor military actions during my lifetime. God help us!

My daughter Julie and my wife Jeanne, arrived at about ten forty five in the morning. She brought me a patriotic looking plant complete with green leaves and red flowers plus a small American flag sticking boldly out of the top. It is "real" so I will have to remember to water it from time to time. They also brought several books and some goodies but not too many. Jeanne helped me and my wheeled walker down the hall and out the side door where Julie was waiting for us. Since it was early, we went to Dollar General first where I loaded up with supplies and more goodies. When I talk to Jeanne by phone, I always talk to Snoopy too. It may seem a little odd to carry on a phone conversation with a cat but Jeanne holds the phone up to Snoopy's ear and I could swear that cat understands every word.

Anyway, I promised to get Snoopy some treats and, according to Jeanne, Snoopy walked away with a smile on her feline face. I kept my word and when Jeanne got back to her assisted living apartment Snoopy was waiting for her promised reward. Cats know!

After our shopping trip we got back into Julie's car and headed for Longhorn Steak House. When we arrived the place was nearly full. Apparently, a lot of veterans were attracted by the free soft drinks and the Texas Tonions. We were seated and the waitress took my wheeled walker and parked it out of the way. This was the day I had been waiting for. I ordered a Flo's filet with a salad and loaded baked potato. Jeanne selected a half rack of ribs and Julie chose the Flo's filet. Both picked salads and baked sweet potatoes with cinnamon and gosh only knows what else. The Tonions arrived first on a long plate with some kind of dip followed by my free coffee, bread, and the girls' water. We chowed down on the Tonions and the bread but before we could consume more than a few bites, the steaks and ribs arrived.

Jeanne let me have a tiny sliver of her ribs in exchange for a much larger chunk of my filet. She only weighs about 120 pounds but boy can she eat! Her whole plate full and whatever she can inveigle off mine. I have heard it said that when a woman eats off your plate she must love you. She must love me a lot because she has done that to me ever since we met nearly fifty years ago. Never gains an ounce either! Disgusting!

Finally we were finished. Stuffed full. The girls asked the waitress for "take out " boxes for the few scraps that remained. Julie grabbed the Tonions that were left for my grandson Cory, who never seems to get full. Poor little fellow! Only 6 foot one and 225 pounds with a Black Belt in Tai Kwon Do. I got the bill and, with Julie's approval, paid the twenty percent tip. The smiling waitress recovered my wheeled walker from wherever she had stashed it and toward the door we went. On the way out I grabbed a handful of peppermints, got into the car, and it was back to Trinka Davis Veterans Village. Julie and Jeanne left about two pm to try to beat the traffic jams on I-20 and I-75. They did. All in all it was a Veterans Day to be remembered. I am looking forward to

Thanksgiving! Whoop De Do!

Today I had surgery for a basal cell carcinoma of my forehead and a squamous cell tumor on my right ear. The dermatology section at Atlanta VAMC in Decatur, had done the biopsy a while back and recommended a doctor some miles from here to do the job. Long rides are very hard on me and I didn't want to have to make several trips back and forth so I asked for and received permission to use my Medicare and AARP supplement to get the surgery from a five star rated doctor right here in Carrollton. Trinka Davis Veteran's Village driver, Arthur Singleton, picked me up about eight am at C-House, and by eight fifteen we were in the office of Dr. David Schoenfeld. Arthur is retired after doing his twenty in the Army plus ten more in the reserves. He was also injured in the service and receives a ninety percent service connected disability. We have a lot in common because, in addition to his military service he is, like me, a Mason.

Dr. Schoenfeld and his nurse were great. Both had a sense of humor and a way of putting you at ease so it seemed more like a friendly visit that a surgical procedure. In short order, he skillfully scraped the basal cell carcinoma off my forehead and attacked the squamous cell tumor on my ear. He sent the ear chunk he had cut out to the lab to make certain he had removed it all and gave me a cup of coffee while we waited for the results. They were positive and the cancers were history! It was there that I learned a dark secret about Amy Dickerson, our LPN, who used to work for him and had told me how good he was. I t seems Amy is also known as the "peanut lady"." Amy was born in Leesburg, Florida and had a job in Orlando. On weekends she worked at another profession, selling boiled peanuts from a stand on the road side. When I got back to C-House I confronted her with the information I had gleaned from the good doctor. Turning a bit red in the face she admitted her past vocation as a boiled peanut peddler. If she was as good at selling peanuts as she is as a nurse she must have led Florida in peanut promotion! Eat your heart out Jimmy Carter!

After returning from my surgical adventure I went to a Resident's Council Meeting to complain about the murderous door on the laundry room that had assaulted both O.W. and myself several times leaving us battered, bleeding, and bruised. The dirty thing will spring upon you without warning and leave it's mark, usually somewhere on your arms. I got a promise of a solution to the dastardly problem from Steven Releford, our CLC Nurse Manager, but I won't hold my breath. I have heard that song before! Actually, Mr. Releford is a pretty good guy and if he doesn't have to get a "go ahead" from those on high, in Atlanta VAMC, there is a likelihood it will be fixed! The rest of the Resident's Council Meeting was devoted to donuts and apple fritters plus some minor issues and a talk by one of our VA Policemen about the need for making certain that no strangers without proper identification enter this facility. Fat chance! We have over a dozen well-armed police officers on duty out here. Most are huge ex-servicemen was look like they could knock out a raging bull with a single blow, plus a bunch of cranky buzzards, of various ages, who have fought in every war since World War II. Thieves and scoundrels beware!

Will wonders never cease! They finally seem to be working on fixing the laundry room door. If they are successful and I say "if", maybe O.W. and I will be able to go in and out of it without the ever pending danger of being constantly assaulted by the darn thing. The reason for the "if" is because fixing something that was installed during original construction is not always a sure thing. The best way to deal with the problem door would be to install buttons inside and out that would open said door when pushed by the resident. Unfortunately, it appears that this may be impossible due to the probability of pipes, electrical wires, or even vents in the adjacent walls that cannot be easily removed. This leaves few options available to correct the problem and weakening the pressure on the door opener so that it will open and close easier may be all that can be done. Will it correct the "arm bashing" problem? Maybe; maybe not. We will just have to wait and see!

Today the nursing students from the University of West Georgia are back in force. Fortunately their nursing instructor is with them and it appears she really knows her business. One student prepared my medicines while the instructor looked on. This is not an easy job for students serving their internships because VA equipment is different.

Your arm band is scanned into the computer and every medication you receive has to be scanned into the computer to match it. This insures residents are given the correct dosages of each medication and prevents errors. Sometimes the computer and scanning equipment can be finicky, especially when the battery that powers the scanner, is low. That happened this morning and the instructor jumped in to show the student how to overcome the problem. Smart lady! Anyway I got my meds and my pain level is down to "bearable"." I wonder what next week has in store?

CHAPTER EIGHT

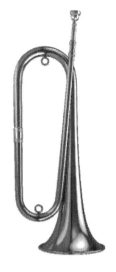

The Staff

Since I have been bragging a lot about the staff at Trinka Davis Veterans Village, CLC in the preceding chapters it is time for me to tell you about them in detail so you can get to know them better. They represent some of the best trained, most competent, most caring folks I have ever met in any VA facility or VA hospital in the whole VA system. And that is saying a lot! I have been so impressed by this facility and the care given residents by its staff that I sent an e-mail to VA Secretary Robert A. McDonald (robert.a.mcdonald@va.gov) praising it. I informed him that I had seen the best and the worst of VA care since I was rated 100 percent service-connected in January 1963 and went on to explain some of the amazing Trinka Davis Veterans Village story. The Secretary e-mailed me a reply which I will always treasure.

In addition to the fine quality of medical and nursing care provided to each of the three "Houses" currently in operation, Trinka Davis Veterans Village Community Living Center offers a wide range of other services for its residents. These include physical therapy and restorative care, psychology, pharmacy, occupational therapy, dietetics, planned recreation, as well as spiritual services (which is optional). I have touched on some of these services in previous chapters, but feel it is necessary to show in greater detail, in a future chapter, just how they interlock with each other to provide each resident with the best quality of life possible.

The nursing staff in each House usually consists of a Registered Nurse, a Licensed Practical Nurse and two Certified Nursing Assistants; seven days a week on each of its two twelve hour shifts. That way residents have full coverage twenty four hours a day. Because requirements differ, the chefs and housekeeping employees in each of the "Houses" work eight hour daytime shifts. When I first moved here in May of 2014, both C-House and A-House had eleven residents each. Since that time "B-House" has opened and is slowly filling up toward its eleven resident capacity. "D-House", which is being designed to care for seriously disabled veterans with memory problems, is expected to open sometime in 2015.

Now that I have gotten through the dry "demographics" of what makes this place tick, the time has come to tell you more about the people who work here, their training, what brought them here, and their future aspirations. All are extremely competent and some are nothing short of amazing. Taking care of a bunch of grizzly, worn out, old war veterans (and a few younger veterans badly disabled by service in more recent wars) is by no means an easy job. For most of the staff this is a "labor of love" and you can see it in their smiles as they walk through the doors at the beginning of their shifts. These are very special people! They really care about each of us and they are glad to be here. During the time I have been here I got to know each one of them personally. To get more information about their backgrounds and aspirations I drew up a "Staff Resume" and asked them to fill it out so I could do them justice when telling their stories. Most did!

One of those very special people is Dr. Jamya Pittman, the Community Living Center's Physician in Charge. Dr. Pittman graduated from the University of Tennessee and is a Board Certified Internist. As such, she must take a test every ten years to retain her Board Certification. She took that test a few weeks ago and, as we all expected, passed with flying colors. Dr. Pittman is one very smart lady! I am kind of partial when it comes to Dr. Pittman as her superb medical ability and quick action has "saved my bacon" more than once. She is also a very compassionate person and cares deeply about her resident patients. It shows!

She is in charge of medical care for residents in "A", "B", and "C"-Houses and how she keeps some of us worn out old veterans functioning day after day seems almost miraculous! I have written quite a bit about this fine lady in previous chapters so I will end my "soliloquy" at this point and get on to the story about another very special person.

Mrs. Mamrom Warner is our Nurse Practitioner for "A", "B", and "C" Houses. She knows her business and she is a whiz at her chosen profession. Today's Nurse Practitioners do much of the same kind of work as General Practice M.D.'s did in the past. Mrs. Warner received her BSN in nursing from Florida State University and her MSM from Emory University. Nurse Practitioners, like Mrs. Warner, add a great deal to the practice of medicine. Their prior "hands on" experience as Registered Nurses has taught them the importance of everyday patient care and their added education in the practice of medicine allows them to be able to treat those patients from both the nurse's and doctor's prospective. In most states Nurse Practitioners are authorized to perform examinations; diagnose medical problems; prescribe most drugs and treatment modalities. They also work in consultation with MD's so the patient gets the best of both worlds.

Mrs. Warner was born in Trinidad. She is a slender, mature, dark skinned lady of deep faith and when I use the word "lady" she fills the bill to a tee. She and her husband have four grown children. When I asked her what brought her to Trinka Davis Veterans Village, CLC, her answer was "The opportunity to work closely with U.S. veterans and make a difference in their lives"." That she has done and done very well. God Bless you, Mrs. Warner. You have certainly succeeded in your carrying out your stated intention. As to her future plans, she hopes to someday travel the world and go on mission trips. She is a credit to her profession.

The next story concerns our eminent psychologist Dr. Patricia Rivera, who I jokingly refer to as being the "dog lady"." Actually, that is meant as a compliment. Dr. Rivera comes to visit me several times a month with her friend "Outlaw" an approximately eighty pound German Shepherd who is the facility's one and only trained "Therapy Dog"." After knocking, they enter my suite together, Outlaw tugging on her leash with Dr. Rivera just behind her with a bed sheet in her hands. Dr. Rivera then tells Outlaw to "sit" while she spreads the sheet over the blankets on my bed as Outlaw waits impatiently nearby. It seems Outlaw sheds quite a bit and the good doctor has a thing about keeping the hair where it can be removed when our visit is over. When the "shed prevention" task is completed Outlaw jumps and with a single bound lands upon my bed, squirms over toward me, and nuzzles my hand. I guess it is her way of saying "Hi"." Obviously, she knows instinctively that I am a dog lover!

I have discovered during a recent "Care Plan" meeting that mine is the only bed Outlaw is allowed on. I feel honored! My wife and I have always had dogs (and cats) during our long marriage and we considered them to be part of our family. Companion animals give unconditional love and that is beyond price! I am somewhat partial to large dogs and our last one "Red" was a combination of Rhodesian Ridgeback and Chow. Red weighed about seventy pounds and under my wife's great care lived to be twenty years old. Her disposition was a lot like Outlaw's, calm and laid back. I have high blood pressure and occasionally suffer from depression. There is something special about a dog, like Outlaw, whose very presence can bring about a feeling of peace. Her lying on my bed just next to me, in my recliner, sometimes licking my hand in friendship, while Dr. Rivera and I talk helps me to view my problems in a different light. Most folks who love dogs will understand what I mean. Dogs rule!

As a psychologist who is trained in geriatrics, Dr. Rivera plays an important part as a member of the treatment team by helping seriously service disabled veterans, like myself, learn to live with chronic pain and disabilities. It helps us to make the best of the strengths we have left and adjust as well as we can to the fact that we can no longer live at home. Sometimes that adjustment can take months. Dr. Rivera is happily married and lives at home with her husband and three dogs, one of whom is a "retired" Therapy Dog. She received her Bachelor's Degree from Mills College in California and her Doctorate from Florida State University in Tallahassee. To simply say she is good at what she does would be putting it too mildly. Actually, she is at the top of her profession and we residents of Trinka Davis Veterans Village, CLC, are fortunate to have her (and Outlaw) caring for us.

There are other professionals in the attached Outpatient Clinic who provide us with a number of very important specialized forms of treatment that will be discussed in detail in a later chapter. But first let me

131

introduce you to the Staff of C-House. These are the people who care for us day and night and they make up a very special treatment team. First, in order of rank come the Registered Nurses closely followed by the Licensed Practical Nurses and then the Certified Nursing Assistants. Each plays an important part in our medical care.

In addition to "fill ins" as the situation requires, C-House has four regular registered nurses. Jamilah Middlebrooks, RN, (aka "Me Me") and Lisa Leonhardt, RN, alternate on the day shift. Ann Wyatt, RN, and Arletha Turner, RN, alternate on the night shift. All four are well trained professionals who practice their chosen professions with a touch of excellence. If someone were to ask me which one was best I simply could not answer. They function as a well matched team and the services they provide to residents is superior. These are four magnificent ladies.

I will tell you about each in turn and let you be the judge as to whom you believe is best. I believe you will find it to be an impossible job!

Jamilah Middlebrooks (aka "Me Me") received her Bachelor's Degree in nursing in Davenport, Iowa. She has an extensive background in psychiatric nursing and long term care which makes her a perfect fit for the kind of residents who live in C-House. Living with serious war time disabilities that can also carry emotional scars can be trying. Nurses who can understand that are a real plus! She does! When I asked what brought her to Trinka Davis Veterans Village, CLC, she

132

told me that "she moved from Dayton, Ohio to Villa Rica, Georgia, because she wanted "to continue her work with veterans"." One of "Me Me's" future goals is to obtain her Doctorate in Nursing to help her move to an executive position where she can work to create change that benefits veterans. She is African American, happily married with two children. "Me Me" does her job with excellence, kindness, and understanding. Who could ask for more? Not me!

Although she started out in a totally different career field, Lisa Leonhardt was born to be a nurse. She is of medium height, blonde, attractive, kind, and compassionate to those she provides care for and her attitude comes from the heart. Prior to going to nursing school at the University of West Georgia, she was employed as a music department buyer for an independent store. When the store closed she decided it was time to make a career change. After receiving her R.N. Degree, and prior to coming to Trinka Davis Veterans Village to work for the Veterans Administration, she spent eight years practicing her profession in a major hospital. She worked here a few months and resigned to take a job at Tanner Memorial Hospital in Carrollton. It was a loss as she was an excellent nurse but, according to her, she preferred to work where there was a greater variety of age groups and medical problems. Handling a bunch of mostly old worn out veterans is not everybody's cup of tea. Good luck in your new job, Lisa. We will miss you!

Sonya Caldwell is a great nurse! She is a petite African

American and just four foot ten inches tall. She is married with two children and she lives in nearby Douglas County. Sonya is very "resident oriented" and looks after her charges like a mother hen. Probably one of the reasons is that she is a disabled veteran herself and understands the resident's problems better than most. She served in Europe at both Granferwhor and K-Town.

After leaving the military Sonya decided on a career in medicine. Her first job was working as a CNA at the VA Medical Center in Fayetteville, North Carolina. Her next step up the ladder was to work as a surgical technician in various facilities and operating rooms. She continued in that position for fifteen years and decide to become an RN. She received her BSN RN Degree at the University of West Georgia and, because she loved surgery, continued to work in various facilities as an Operating Room Nurse. Eventually she came to Trinka Davis Veterans Village because it gave her the opportunity to serve fellow veterans. She was also motivated by the fact that it was close to home and because the VA offers great benefits and opportunities. Her next step toward the top of her profession will be to obtain her Master's Degree in Nursing and work in Case Management or teach Nursing. After getting to know her I have no doubt that she will succeed. She is one very special person!

Ann Wyatt, RN is a slender, medium tall blonde with an engaging personality. She was born in Salisbury, North

Carolina. She holds both a BSN in nursing from Georgia State University in Atlanta and a BA in business administration from Lenoir-Rhyne University, in Hickory, North Carolina. Having served as a flight attendant for eighteen years before retirement she is an experienced traveler whose myriad flights took her all across the USA and around the world many times. She says her favorite domestic city is Seattle and her favorite international city is Dublin, Ireland. The fact that her focus was always on the safety of the flying public has been carried over to the nursing profession as she has made resident safety and resident care a priority. At Trinka Davis Veterans Village, CLC, it is her main concern and she focuses on it with laser like precision. I have come to think of her as "by the book" and, Ann, I mean that as high compliment! If you have an emergency need she is the kind of nurse you want at your side "Johnny on the spot"." She is competent, reassuring, and "cool as a cucumber" under pressure.

When I questioned Ann as to what brought her to Trinka Davis Veterans Village her answer put a lump in my throat. She stated "it was a great opportunity to serve our veterans and thank them in person for their service and sacrifice to the country"." She went on to tell me that "As an RN, TDVV provides a great work and learning environment" and "Every day is full of surprises and challenges!" What a great answer! Questioned as to her future goals, Ann replied that nursing is her "final career path" as she is "winding down her professional life and feels very fortunate to have worked in two dynamic fields: nursing and aviation"." She pointed out that the two are very much alike in that the primary focus is "helping people"."

Ann Wyatt is a person who believes it is an honor and a privilege to work for the VA health care systems and she intends "to spend her final working years helping veterans achieve their personal health goals because it is very special and meaningful to her"." Because Ann Wyatt stated her beliefs and feelings so succinctly, I ended up quoting her almost exactly as she said it and in many cases "word for word"." I have never heard better answers. She lives in Newnan, Georgia and loves cats. As a cat lover myself I can relate to that. And, although she would probably be the last to admit it, she is a great nurse and a person well worth knowing.

Arletha Shanta Turner, RN, is one of my favorite people. I like to think of her as "my good luck charm"." A diminutive lady with African American roots she stands about ten feet tall when it comes to her ability in the nursing profession. She is good! The reason I think of her as my "good luck charm" is because she and CNA Juanita Kirk are the ones who took me to Atlanta VAMC from Trinka Davis Veterans Village, CLC that day in July, 2014 when I had cataract surgery on my right eye. They were there when I went in surgery and were still there talking with my wife Jeanne and our daughter Julie, when I came out.

As I have pointed out previously, the Atlanta VAMC

Eye Clinic had been treating me for years and because I had only one eye, surgery to improve the 20/150 vision in the remaining eye carried some risk. To compound the problem, I have dry macular degeneration plus some retinal scarring. The outcome of the surgery to attempt to improve my vision was somewhat doubtful. The fact that I unexpectedly recovered almost perfect vision was amazing! Arletha Turner is a woman of faith and I have a hunch a prayer or two was said on my behalf. She is that kind of person! Hence the "good luck charm" label. Prayer is a powerful thing!

Arletha Turner was born in Carrollton, Georgia. At thirty four she is one of the youngest RN's in C-House. She previously worked as a Registered Nurse at Piedmont Hospital in Newnan, Georgia; Tanner Medical Center in Villa Rica and in the Home Health Care field. Arletha came to Trinka Davis Veterans Village sort of by accident as she was already gainfully employed at a major hospital. She heard about the opportunity at the VA from a fellow employee, applied for the job and got it. Her future goal is to go back to school and become a Nurse Practitioner. Currently she lives in Temple, Georgia with her three children, two boys and one girl. She is one determined little lady and I predict she will end up at the very top of her field. Go girl - go! Shoot for the moon. Become a Nurse Practitioner! If anyone can make it you can!

C-House at Trinka Davis Veterans Village is served by two excellent full time Licensed Practical Nurses, Amy

Dickerson and Joseph ("Big Joe") Hosier, both of whom alternate with each other on the day shift. As of the time of this writing, there are no "full time" Licensed Practical Nurses on the night shift but, when necessity demands extra help, an LPN usually comes over from one of the other houses. Generally, that is Kimberly Chambers a fine, well trained, African American LPN, who knows her business.

At Trinka Davis Veterans Village LPNs concentrate on passing out medications and such other medical care as is required. It is a busy job as most residents must take their medications within a specific ""two hour" time frame. I get my meds (consisting of a total of about twenty pills) at nine am, three pm and nine pm plus puffing on an inhaler at seven am, noon, and seven pm. The ten other residents in C-House must also be medicated, many on different time frames than mine. All medications must be dispensed by an LPN or an RN and checked and computer logged to prevent errors. Not an easy task if it is done correctly. And at our facility it is - every time!

Joseph ("Big Joe") Hosier received his LPN Degree at Rock Valley College in Illinois. In addition to being a trained LPN, he is a masseur who can take the kinks out of your spine in a millisecond. He is also a former Marine who served four years in country during Desert Storm and in Panama during the time of the Noriega removal. He has service connected injuries and has applied for disability compensation which is currently being considered by the Veterans Administration.

Joe has an extensive background in nursing is and he

138

is the best of the best. Prior to coming to Trinka Davis Veterans Village, CLC he worked in Orthopedics at St. Anthony's Medical Center for three years; Unihealth Post-Acute Care in Fairburn, Georgia and at Alpine Fireside in Rockford, Illinois.

Joe Hosier is married. He and his wife have a ten year old son. They live in Newnan, Georgia, about thirty miles from Trinka Davis Veterans Village. Joe and his son like Werther's Original hard candy and he is a major consumer from the goodie bowl that I keep filled on my moveable tray for my second family, the staff. I am the one who tacked the nickname "Big Joe" on him because he is a large man and as strong as a bull. I have a propensity for falling on occasion and when that happens I can't get up. Sound like a certain TV ad? Anyway, on two of my falling occasions, two female CNAs tried their best to get me back on my feet without success. When it began to look like I was stuck on the floor, until someone found a derrick, Joe Hosier came into my room and, despite his injuries, lifted me off the floor like picking up a baby. He sat me down and began to repair my injuries as if it was nothing at all. From that time forward he was "Big Joe" and he can have all the Werther's candy he (and his son) can eat.

Joe Hosier's reason for coming to Trinka Davis Veterans Village, CLC, was that he wanted to work with seriously service disabled veterans because he could relate to their situation. He hopes that someday he can get a job with the CDC or with the VA Community Based Outpatient Clinic in Newnan. He is a great cook and I believe he would be a great success if he opened a restaurant where he could cook and become an even bigger "Big Joe"." Gotcha!

Licensed Practical Nurse Amy Dickerson and her husband live in Whitesburg, Georgia, whose 2010 population was estimated to be 588. Apparently, it is a good place to raise children as Amy has a brood that includes two boys, two girls, and two stepdaughters. She comes from a family with a history of producing both men and women who served our country going back to the day her father was drafted into the Army and served in Vietnam. Amy's husband also served in the Army during Desert Storm/Desert Shield. Their son, Joshua is currently in the Marine Corps and one of her daughters and husband spent five years in the Marine Corps, where both were deployed to Afghanistan. A lifetime of exposure to family members who served in the military and became "her heroes" played a prominent part in her decision to bring her nursing skills to Trinka Davis Veterans Village, CLC. And "nursing skills" she has in abundance!

LPN Amy Dickerson was born in Leesburg, Florida. She is a slender, attractive, medium tall, blond lady who received her LPN Degree from West Georgia Technical College in Carrollton, Georgia. A long, varied work history over several years, has provided her with invaluable medical experience in the fields of Dermatology, Ear, Nose, and Throat, Ob/Gyn, and Correctional nursing. When asked what brought her to Trinka Davis Veterans Village, CLC, her answer was "this is my way of serving our veterans"." She is an outstanding nurse, a credit to the VA, who plans on furthering her education to become an RN. She also has a past vocation that is both interesting and unusual and I found out about it in a purely unexpected manner.

I had a basal cell carcinoma on my forehead and a squamous cell tumor on my right earlobe. I needed surgery but didn't want to make the long trip to Atlanta VAMC because it is hard on me and it takes me a couple of days to recover. I wanted to get surgery closer to "home" and had both Medicare and a supplement that would pay for it so I mentioned it to Amy, not realizing that she had worked for a local dermatologist. She told me about Dr. David Schoenfeld, who owns West Georgia Dermatology and was her former employer. I went and discovered that he was not only a "Five Star" dermatologist he was also a fountain of information and he shared Amy's deep, dark, secret with me. It seems that Amy was known as the "peanut lady" because she boiled peanuts at home and sold them by the roadside in Orlando, Florida. I confronted her with my little gem and, somewhat abashed, she admitted her former vocation. She then informed me that it had been a lucrative venture making her more money in two days that her regular job paid in a week. I wonder if I could set up a "boiled peanut" stand outside Trinka Davis Veterans Village? Stay with us Amy. You are not only a great nurse, you are also a bundle of laughs!

Certified Nursing Assistants play a very important part in the care given to the residents of Trinka Davis Veterans Village, CLC. They conduct "finger stick "tests to monitor blood sugar levels; check blood pressures; oxygen levels and take temperatures which I guess are what doctors refer to as "vital signs"." In addition, CNAs accompany residents on trips for medical appointments at Atlanta VAMC, as well as VA van trips to restaurants, stores, and other functions outside the CLC to handle emergencies and provide assistance to disabled residents. Thoroughly trained CNAs are a "vital" part of the operation of VA Hospitals, Clinics, and Community Living Centers, like Trinka Davis Veterans Village. The Veterans Administration also requires that their CNAs receive a level of training considerably more extensive than that required by most other medical facilities. As a result, their pay scales, and benefit packages are generally much higher. And now, on with the stories of the awesome CNAs who work in C-House!

Nikki Morris is just twenty eight years old and medium tall, with lovely dark brown hair. Born in China Grove, North Carolina, she lives in Carrollton, Georgia with her husband and two and a half children. That number will increase to three in a just a few more months. Nikki currently holds certifications as a Certified Nursing Assistant and as a Phlebotomist in both the states of Georgia and North Carolina. She is a "workaholic" and one of the best CNAs I have ever seen. Nothing stops her and nothing is too difficult for her. Not even tying knots in the ends of our "full size" bottom sheets so they can be made to fit our three quarter beds. If you think that is easy...try it! Nikki is special!

Nikki Morris worked at a number of different jobs before coming to Trinka Davis Veterans Village, CLC. Starting her working experience with a cleaning company, she moved into restaurant food service and finally, into nursing which has turned out to be her true vocation. She was made for it and took to it like a "duck takes to water"." When asked what brought her to Trinka Davis Veterans Village, her answer was "I am blessed to be able to care for our veterans"." The truth of the matter is that we seriously service disabled "veterans" are blessed to have Nikki taking care of us. She does a superb job!

As to the question of what her future goals were, she explained that while she hoped to go back to school to study radiology and ultra sound and possibly work in the women's clinic at the VA. She also told me that being a CNA is very rewarding, that she enjoys the position she is currently in and that she also enjoys being a mother. If anyone can juggle all three of the above at the same time it is Nikki Morris! One tough lady!

Teresa Easter has one of the most unusual life stories I have ever heard in more than eighty seven years of living and I have heard a lot! Born in Morganfield, Kentucky, she was the daughter of a coal miner. Strike that and make it a "coal mineress"." It was her mother who worked in the mines and who did so until she retired. One of the first such instances in Kentucky and probably in the entire USA. Teresa's skin is almost the color of dark honey and her heritage is a combination of both African American and Cherokee Native American. Her high cheekbones are classic Indian. I know because my maternal great grandmother was a full blooded Chickasaw who married my Caucasian great grandfather. Her Native American features and her skin color were passed down to my maternal grandmother and my mother, the latter lightening a bit on the way due to dilution. I am proud to have a squirt or two of Native American blood in my veins and for some reason can almost always spot it in others.

In addition to being a Certified CNA, Teresa Easter is certified in both Human Services and Mental Health. She has worked in nursing for twenty four years, eleven and a half of those with the State of Virginia Mental Institute. That should serve her well here at Trinka Davis Veterans Village as some of us can act a little "wacky" at times and we need someone around who understands us. Teresa fills the bill! Soft spoken and always smiling, with a sense of humor and a calming attitude, she is great to be around. She transferred here from Atlanta VAMC to take a full time position at Trinka Davis Veterans Village, CLC, and we hope she stays. I believe she will because she enjoys working with veterans. A glutton for punishment? Just kidding Teresa! We love you just the way you are!

Morris Flowers is a tall, husky, forty four year old

African American who has years of experience as a Certified Nursing Assistant. He has been with the VA for nearly eighteen of those years and really knows his profession. Nine years of that time was spent working at the VA in New Jersey and eight and a half years with the Atlanta VAMC in Decatur, Georgia, He is also a former Marine who sustained a service connected disability from injuries while he was in the Corps.

Wanting a "change of pace" in his life for himself and his family, Morris relocated to Temple, Georgia with his wife and five children (three girls and two boys) and joined the Staff at C-House in Trinka Davis Veterans Village. It was a "win win" for both himself and us residents as he brought a large store of knowledge gained over many years as a Veterans Administration CNA along with him. And that is a plus! I got to know Morris Flowers when he started performing blood sugar tests and vital signs readings on me. He is intelligent, has a sense of humor and can relate to and communicate well with the residents, partly because of his service and partly because of his exemplary character.

As to his future hopes and dreams, Morris loves to cook. He wants to "one day open a restaurant that caters a wide variety of cuisines to people all over"." Tomorrow is Thanksgiving Day and he is having some twenty family members (some from as far away as New Jersey) at his home for the feast. He told me that he himself is baking three cakes and his wife and mother-in-law are baking six pies to go along with myriads of other tasty dishes. When I inquired as to his address he told me "just follow the smell"." Probably figured (correctly) that I would show up and eat too much of his goodies if he told me his address.

I wonder if Dr. Rivera could be persuaded to lend me "Outlaw", the therapy dog, for the day? I understand dogs have a sense of smell five hundred times as sharp as we humans. I'll bet Morris would be shocked if we tracked him down and showed up on his doorstep ready to eat! Maybe he will save me a piece of one of the cakes he is baking and a turkey leg for Outlaw? Probably not!

James Johnson is a tall, lean, twenty nine year old African American who was born in Mobile, Alabama. He received his Certificate as a Certified Nursing Assistant at age eighteen from the Earl C. Clements Job Corps and has worked at his profession for the past eleven years. The Earl C. Clements Job Corp. is administered by the Department of Labor and is the nation's largest residential and educational program for opportunity seeking youth. James has a vast amount of nursing experience in the fields of geriatrics, cardiovascular, and mental health care and really knows his business. He has only been at C-House, in Trinka Davis Veterans Village for a short time but his personality and ability makes him a perfect fit for the job. He is single and now resides in Carrollton, Georgia.

When I asked James what brought him to Trinka Davis Veterans Village he replied that he had wanted to move to Georgia but could not find work there so "he prayed for a secure job with a stable income"." Two weeks later he was contacted by a company that supplied contract employees to the VA and was offered a temporary position as a CNA, at Atlanta VAMC! We should never underestimate the power of prayer! He worked there for a year, first in mental health and finally in Eagle's Nest, the Atlanta VA's Nursing Home. It was there he met CNA Morris Flowers who had just applied for a transfer to Trinka Davis Veterans Village. Morris told James about the opening and he also applied for a transfer there. Ten minutes after he applied the applications were closed. He got the job by a whisker!

As to his future goals, James wants to continue his education to become a Mortician and after graduating, to go on to college and earn his Bachelor's Degree. I suggested he talk to C.B., my next door neighbor, who has two Purple Hearts from wounds during World War II and later became a Mortician who owned his own Funeral Home in Etowah, Tennessee for many years.

You have what it takes to succeed in life, James! Go for it young man and don't let anything stop you! You have already proved you can do anything you set your mind to!

There are three other CNAs who work in C-House and all are extremely competent. Two, Jamal Robinson and Heather Lewis, alternate on the night shift while the third, Juanita Kirk, works the day shift. Jamal is twenty five years old, a tall African American, and a senior at the University of West Georgia. He is intelligent, very efficient, has a positive attitude and makes every move count. He is due to receive his Bachelor's Degree shortly and will undoubtedly go on to be successful in his future endeavors. Jamal has what it takes! Heather Lewis is dark blonde in her twenties, of medium height, and is expecting her first child in a few months. She is good at her job and always on schedule. Right now she is "walking on clouds" as she and the love of her life are hoping for a daughter.

Juanita Kirk is married, with four children and is African American with Cherokee blood from her forebears. Attractive, experienced, and smart, she is one of the top CNAs at Trinka Davis Veterans Village, CLC. Like RN Lisa Leonhardt, she has a fondness for small dark chocolate Hershey bars. When I buy a mixed bag containing a variety of the little yummies I try to pick out the dark ones and save them so I can divide them between her and Lisa. Juanita often is assigned to train new incoming CNAs which takes her to other "Houses" and we do not see as much of her as we used to. She is the CNA that drove me to Atlanta VAMC for my July surgery and with RN Arletha Turner, stayed outside the operating room talking with my wife and daughter until my surgery was over. She is a very special person in my book.

There is one thing that nearly all the staff members I have written about in this Chapter have in common. When you ask each of them why they came here their answer is always almost identical. They came here to help veterans! It seems almost as if some powerful "Unseen Hand" intentionally directed their combined paths to Trinka Davis Veterans Village because it realized how much we seriously service disabled veterans needed the understanding and wonderful care they provide. They make a real and important difference in the quality of our lives. They truly are our "second family"!

CHAPTER NINE

Friends and Allies

November 27, 2014 is Thanksgiving Day and the start of another glorious Holiday season. Families gather from all over to share the festivities and to celebrate the meaning of the day. It is a day filled with happiness and wonder and it propels us toward the annual Christmas Day culmination that almost ends the year. Several of the heartier residents of C-House at Trinka Davis Veterans Village who are still physically able to travel have already been picked up by their family members and are either at, or headed for, their destinations. They will be in cozy homes where platters of good food awaits hungry bellies and where, once again, they will share scads of love and laughter with treasured family members. I wish each of them a wonderful day, a day filled with memories they can carry with them when they return to the routine of VA nursing home living.

Some of us, myself included, will never be able to go home again to share Thanksgiving with our loved ones. Our days for that are over and all we have left are the memories of happier times in the past. This will be my first Thanksgiving away from my family in nearly half a century. I feel a sense of loss and it makes me very sad. I think that feeling is probably shared by all residents of this facility that are unable to go home. On the bright side, our chefs are preparing an allegedly sumptuous Thanksgiving dinner for those of us who are unable to leave and we are allowed to invite a couple of folks we care about to join us in the meal.

I really should not be complaining. My daughter Sandy and her husband Tom, came to see me just two days ago after making the four and a half hour drive from north Florida just to visit and take me to lunch at the Lazy Donkey Mexican Restaurant and to help me shop for necessities and goodies at a nearby CVS. Tom has a large, new, extended cab Ford short bed truck and he brought along a footstool so I could, with his help, step up to get inside. I had a surprise for my daughter that told her how very much I love her. It was an oval shaped pendant with ten small diamonds on the front hanging from a beautiful eighteen inch chain. Engraved on the back it was circled with the words "My little girl yesterday; my friend today; my daughter forever"." Down the center, on three carved hearts were the words, "I Love You"." The look on her face was worth a million dollars!

We, the residents who had to stay behind, were served our Thanksgiving dinner in the Fred Kelley Clubhouse. Some of the residents had invited friends or relatives and it was packed solid! The food was fair but plentiful and it was prepared and served with loving hands. Although it wasn't the same as being home with family, Thanksgiving Day at

Trinka Davis Veterans Village went pretty well. There were a couple of serious disappointments however and they affected two C-House residents considerably. The first happened to L.B. who was expecting his family to come to take him home to share Thanksgiving Dinner with them. Although he waited anxiously, they did not show and they did not even bother to call. It hurt him deeply and it showed. My heart went out to him and I did my best to cheer him up. He ate Thanksgiving dinner with the rest of us, in the Fred Kelley Clubhouse, but left early to return to C-House. I wonder if his family realizes the pain their absence caused him. Neglect by your loved ones is hard to bear.

The second incident concerns ninety five year old W.J. After the bird feeder incident seemed to have been resolved so he could continue to have close access to fill his outside bird feeders, according to him, another attempt has been made to take this pleasure away from him. It is my understanding that W.J. twice placed a sign on the fire door that referred to Trinka Davis Veterans Village, CLC, as a "Controlled Living Center" and that a VA police officer saw him do it and took photos of the event. W.J. claims the officer told him they had enough on him to have him thrown out of the facility. The police here are generally a pretty nice bunch of fellows and I wonder if the officer had orders from someone else to take this action or if actually was as W.J. claimed. If so, perhaps that individual had better read Title 38, US Code 1710, Section 1710A, relating to a resident's rights before making a move in this direction. It might prevent a messy lawsuit and a lot of undeserved bad publicity.

This petty brouhaha has W.J. so visibly upset to the point that I fear the problem may adversely affect his health. It would seem to me that a simple solution would be to have one of the police officers escort him in and out of the door in question a couple of times daily so he could fill his feeders. It would also restore one of the few real enjoyments this elderly, wheelchair bound, World War II veteran still has left to give his life meaning. Is that little bit of kindness too much to ask?

Sunday my daughter Julie is bringing my wife Jeanne and my son-in-law, Tom, to visit and take me to lunch. Hopefully, one or both of my grandsons can come with them. I purchased an identical oval shaped pendant for Julie, like the one I gave Sandy, and cannot wait to see her reaction when I present it to her. I love my daughters very much and want them to know it so when I pass on they will have visible symbols of that love to remember me by. No father ever had better, more caring, daughters. I really hit the jackpot! Twice!

Having two daughters with husbands bearing the same first name may be a bit unusual but I have solved the problem by calling Julie's husband "Thomas Edward" and Sandy's husband "Thomas Richard" when they are both present at the same time. I feel very blessed to have two such wonderful son-in-laws. I also need to come up with some kind of memento to give my stepdaughter, Cheryl. She is very precious to me but they don't seem to make pendants like these with wording that fits stepdaughters. I will just have to keep looking for something that conveys the way I feel about her. As I love her dearly, I wouldn't want her to feel left out.

The bird feeding issue I previously reported is getting to be hilarious! Old W.J. continues to sneak out the fire door near his suite and load his feeders to supply his feathered friends. He looks both ways, quickly stuffs a slim pillow in place to block the door latch so he can get back inside and out he goes lickety split, power chair in high gear. Some of W.J.'s fellow bird lovers are complicit in providing him with left over portions of their bread and one, who shall remain nameless, even let him back in through the door when he inadvertently locked himself out. I have a hunch some of the VA policemen know what is going on and are probably turning a blind eye. After all, two years have passed since this facility was constructed and an alarm still hasn't been installed on the fire door. Trinka Davis Veterans Village is a wonderful place that does a terrific job to help seriously service disabled veterans, like W.J. The last thing it needs is some buffoon causing it to receive undeserved bad publicity over such a harmless activity by threatening a one hundred percent service disabled ninety five year old World War II veteran with expulsion over something so petty.

Sunday rolled around and my family arrived about eleven am. Julie, Tom, my oldest grandson, Neil and my sweet wife Jeanne came into the door of my suite like a bunch of wise

154

men bearing gifts. Only there weren't "three" like in the Christmas story, there were four and two of them were female. Julie began to unpack what turned out to be "Christmas treasures" and the decoration of my digs began in earnest. Out came a poinsettia, an artificial lighted Christmas tree and a large Santa Claus standing over a smaller Santa Claus. All of the above found homes on the large countertop that extends the length of my bedroom and which holds, among myriads of other things, my computer and printer. Stickers designating the "season" were affixed to my window and a lighted "Merry Christmas" was hung on my back bedroom wall. Finally, a lighted Christmas wreath was hung in my bathroom to the left of my large mirror and the job of turning my suite into a "Christmas Miracle" was complete. Wow!

I sat back, admiring their handiwork for a few minutes; got up from my recliner; wheeled over to the top drawer beneath the countertop and took out the box containing an identical necklace and pendant exactly like the one I had given Sandy a few days before. I handed it to Julie. She opened it; read the engraving on the back; removed the necklace she was wearing and after giving me a hug, put it on. The look on her face said everything. Now I had two daughters who would always know how much their father loved them. I also have a similar "surprise" coming for my wife Jeanne, which I expect to give her on their next trip to visit me.

It was getting near lunch time so we loaded into Julie's Toyota Venza and headed for our mutual choice of the day,

Longhorn. We arrived shortly before the "church crowd" and were seated around a large table with room beside it for my rolling walker. We ordered our meal. For the girls it was strawberry chicken salad (no weight gain permitted); Tom had his usual, salmon; Neil chose a rib eye (medium) and I settled for ground round with mushrooms and onion sticks. Before we were through with our meal the "church crowd" had arrived in force and the place was packed! We capped off the trip with a stop at Dollar General where I could replenish my waning supplies (mostly goodies) and where Jeanne dropped in a couple of bags of cat treats to take to her assisted living apartment for Snoopy.

Snoopy is our plump, orange and white inside feline who probably weighs fifteen pounds by now due to the oversupply of the tasty yummies she begs from Jeanne who cannot seem to say "no" to her. As I reported before, my nightly phone conversations with my wife also includes a short "talk" with Snoopy who seems to listen intently to every word I say. Once in a while she answers with a "Meow" or at least I think it is an answer. I sometimes wonder what her response would be if I forgot to send home the apparently expected cat treats. I have a feeling she would let me know in no uncertain terms. She loves my wife and makes a great companion for her to help ease the pain we both feel from separation.

December first has arrived and the final days of 2014

are waning rapidly. Last night, an ambulance came here to haul R.M. to Tanner Medical Center's Emergency Room. We residents always dread it when something like that happens and wonder if the "haulee" will make it back to his room or if his time has come. I first realized that R.M. had made it back, this time, when I saw one of the CNAs going into his room with the finger sticking equipment from my seat at the breakfast table. Like me, R.M. is a diabetic. He is also, like me, in his late eighties. We all heaved a sigh of relief and returned to our food with gusto. R.M. is well liked and he would have been sorely missed!

RN Ann Wyatt came by this morning and had to puncture me twice to get a couple of vials of blood for testing. That is unusual as Ann generally gets it on the "first try" but I am dehydrated to the point that my veins don't pop up like they usually do. After she left, I got on my computer to report the goings on at C-House and afterward had one of the CNAs, Juanita Kirk, help me into the zippered leg sleeves so I could spend an hour with my compression pump. That usually reduces the swelling somewhat and drops my blood pressure to help prepare me for the day. I had no sooner removed the leg sleeves when Victor, the head of Restorative Care, came by to take me for my daily walk with my rolling walker. We didn't go the usual distance as yesterday's outing with my family left me with a high pain level and severely swollen legs. I guess I will have to take the manual wheelchair that folds with me for future outings because it is getting too difficult and too painful to use my rolling walker any more. As they say "Old age is not for sissies"!

Today was a day for a "Kroger" shopping trip. Kroger in Carrollton has plenty of electric carts on hand to satisfy the needs of the entire Trinka Davis Veterans Village, CLC brigade. The CNAs, and the driver of the big VA van, round the carts up, bring them to the residents who struggle to get on board, and it is "off to the races"." From that point on, it is "zip here and grab" "zip there and grab" until the cart baskets are chock full of enough desired treasures to last until the next trip. While Kroger is basically a grocery store and doesn't carry quite the variety of goods that Wal-Mart does, it does have most of the things necessary to provide for our "day to day" needs. Also, we disabled veterans don't have to compete as hard for electric carts. Most Kroger shoppers are there looking for groceries instead of wildly plowing through aisles, like at Wal-Mart, and riding in electric carts some don't need, in desperate search of Christmas "bargains"." Since I had loaded up at Dollar General the day before, I stayed home. One of my "smarter" moves!

It is December 2, 2014, the day I have been impatiently waiting for. At eleven am this very morning my Dermatologist, Dr. Schoenfeld, is scheduled to remove the stitches from my right ear that he put in after he removed a squamous cell tumor eighteen days ago. My biggest problem was trying to find someone to take me from Trinka Davis Veterans Village to his office in Carrollton and it looked for a while like it wasn't going to happen. C-House (and the other two Houses) were understaffed with a single RN, a couple of LPNs, and several CNAs covering all three. Part of the reason for the staff shortage was the resignation of RN Lisa Leonhardt who left on Thanksgiving Day to take an offer she couldn't refuse at Tanner Medical Center. She will be missed as she was a great nurse.

To further compound my transportation problem, the nearby exit door that I had formerly been using to save steps was blocked and I am unable to make more than short trips with my rolling walker due to severe pain and weakness in my legs and back. To say I was sweating bullets about how I was going to get there on time would be putting it mildly! The minutes flew by until a solution finally dawned upon the remaining crew. The problem was solved by CNA Juanita Kirk who grabbed a manual wheelchair from C.H.'s suite; plunked my rear in it and pushed me the entire distance through the long halls to the loading area far in front of the main entrance. Mrs. Reeves, a CNA from one of the other Houses, followed behind with my rolling walker. The transfer from manual wheelchair to car took place at the loading area when yet another CNA, a young lady named Alafia, pulled up in a small Ford government vehicle, of undetermined age, and helped me into the front seat while Juanita Kirk wiggled my walker into the back seat. We arrived at Dr. Schoenfeld's office on the stroke of eleven. Wow! That was close! Thank God for those wonderful CNAs!

From then on it was all gravy. The stitches were removed; the basal cell carcinoma on my forehead was examined and twenty minutes after our arrival at the good doctor's office we were back in the small Ford headed toward Trinka Davis Veterans Village. When we got there, I shuffled down the long yellow brick path to the front entrance slowly pushing my rolling walker as best I could. VA Police Officer Magee (who is larger than the average NFL Linebacker) opened the front door and down I plopped on the nearest bench. Officer Magee noticed the manual wheelchair from my original trip was still where it had been parked. He pointed it out to Alafia, the attractive young African American CNA who had driven me to my appointment. I was loaded back into the wheelchair and pushed by the same CNA for the rest of the trip back to C-House. Officer Magee followed with my rolling walker. He looked like a giant pushing a toothpick with wheels! Talk about teamwork! These folks are amazing!

Christmas Day will be here in just three short weeks and, like Thanksgiving, I won't be able to spend it with my family. I will also miss the Advent Season when my church, St. Clements Episcopal, in Canton lights candles in the Advent wreath, one on each Sunday until Christmas arrives. The feeling of love and joy and the many activities and festivities that take place as the season winds down toward the Great Day of Celebration has always warmed my heart. Realizing that these days are over for me is understandable but hard to swallow. Unfortunately, that is the way the cookie crumbles.

Some of my sense of loss will be offset by the fact that my family will come to visit me and we will be able to celebrate be it a few days early or a few days late. Thank God for my wonderful daughters, sons-in-law, and my grandsons. They remain "close" and I feel truly blessed.

This morning breakfast was a treat for a change! Leonard Mack (known to us as "Mack") is the Chef and he prepared an omelet that was to die for. Mine was loaded with tasty tomatoes and mushrooms and done exactly to my taste. With two strips of crisp bacon and hash browns for a side it made my day. "Mack" is an African American disabled veteran, not overly tall and wears a smile that matches his cooking ability. Prior to coming to Trinka Davis Veterans Village, CLC, he was a professional Chef who cooked at some of the top Buckhead restaurants where the food is great and the prices are through the roof! I have heard for the umpteenth time, that our facility may be hiring a total of eight Chefs, two for each House. I hope we residents, at C-House, are fortunate enough to get both "Mack" and Tamika Miller. The current "so so" cooking, especially at dinner, would improve one hundred percent! They can make a hamburger taste like a prime filet. Dream on, old man!

Today is Saturday and as I look out my window, I can see the rain is heartily pouring down. Some of the guys in C-House went to a breakfast put on monthly by American Legion Post 143. Not being a "duck" I passed. Hope they don't get too soaked getting in and out of the big VA van! Several VFW members just dropped into my suite, gave me some nice gifts, and informed me that a Post is going to be started in the near future, right here at Trinka Davis Veterans Village. They also left me some sugar free candy which I will consume shortly with deep appreciation for their thoughtfulness. As a former VFW member, who dropped out because I moved to an area where there was no Post, I will probably rejoin here.

I have charged up my power wheel chair so I can attend today's Christmas program sponsored by the Amvets. It is going to be held partly in "A-House" and partly at the Fred Kelley Clubhouse, which is right across the hall. The first part will be held at "A-House" because it has more room for the Exhibition Drill. It will be put on by the Carrollton High School Air Force JROTC Cadets who need sufficient space to move around. I have it on good authority that they will giving out some early Christmas gifts and luscious goodies after the program and I wouldn't want the chair's batteries to die on the way over there. It would be tough to be stuck in the hall while everyone else is watching the entertainment and stuffing themselves.

Lunch was over and 12:45 P.M. rolled around so I got in my power chair and headed for "A-House", hoping to get a prime location to watch the action from. I did!

A very pretty lady came up to where I had parked, introduced herself as "Pam" and informed me she had been assigned to help me for the event. She sat down next to me. The show began with a sterling performance by the Carrollton

High School Air Force JROTC Cadets Exhibition Drill team led by Master Sergeant Marvin Cox. They were great! Every move was executed to perfection. It was thrilling to watch a group of high school kids do a job that would have pleased even the toughest Drill Sergeant! They were followed by another team of JROTC Cadets who put on a rifle drill using what appeared to be 1903 Springfield rifles. It was nothing short of amazing the way they handled themselves and their rifles. If some of them decide on a military career our country will be well served.

When the Cadet drills were over, we moved out of "A-House" and went directly across the hall to the Fred Kelley Clubhouse for the rest of the program. It began with a moving Presentation of the Colors and the Pledge of Allegiance followed by the National Anthem. My cap was over my heart and a lump rose into my throat as the patriotic words and stirring music echoed through the room. After an Invocation by Chris Williams of Amvets 118, the Carrollton High School Show Choir, directed by Mr. Tommy Cox sang Christmas songs and hymns that brought back memories of Holiday celebrations long gone by. Mine were not the only eyes in the room that shed a tear or two. The program concluded with the distribution of soft drinks, loads of cupcakes, cookies, brownies and other toothsome sweets which were consumed by the residents in record time.

Pam, the nice lady who was my conductor for the day, helped me back to my suite with two large bags full of gifts which included copy paper for my printer and white chocolate truffles. I also brought back a plate full of goodies for future consumption for when my blood sugar drops a bit. I have a hunch it is through the roof from the act of gluttony I performed at the Fred Kelley Clubhouse but I simply could not help myself. Everything looked (and was) so good. "Pam" is an officer and longtime member of the Amvets Auxiliary and her husband has served for many years as an officer of the Amvets. What a great group of people they are! Volunteers like these folks make life a lot more pleasant for those of us seriously disabled veterans who live at Trinka Davis Veterans Village, CLC. We appreciate knowing we are not forgotten. Today was a day to be remembered.

When I wrote "today was a day to be remembered" I wasn't far off the mark. CNA Juanita Kirk came in about 4:30 pm to check my blood sugar. She rammed the needle punch into my finger and we waited for the results as the meter ticked toward the answer. It was 307! My sin of gluttony at the Christmas Party had caught up with me. Anything over 300 means a shot of insulin in the belly. Juanita "ratted me out" and LPN Amy Dickerson came it to my suite, syringe and needle in hand. I unbuckled my belt and exposed my tummy. Zap! It burned a little as the juice shot in which was probably what I deserved for pigging out. After some deep thought and with much reluctance I gave the balance of goodies left on my plate to Amy. I knew if I kept them I would eat them as I have little will power where sweets are concerned. However, as there are several more Christmas Parties, scheduled by other volunteer groups, prior to Christmas I will probably "sin again" and have to pay the price for my transgressions. Oh, well! Christmas only comes once a year! And it really didn't hurt that bad.

Today is December seventh and the seventy third anniversary of the day of the Japanese attack on Pearl Harbor. I will always remember that awful Sunday in 1941 when our table top radio blared out the dreadful news. We were living in Akron, Ohio and I was a boy of just fourteen and a half, too young to fight but old enough to want to. I remember the tone of President Roosevelt's voice as he told the country "this is a date that will live in infamy"." Today, at Trinka Davis Veterans Village, CLC there was no "Ceremony of Remembrance" in honor of the thousands of lives that were lost on that fateful day. There was only silence from those of us old enough to remember. And maybe that "silence" is a fitting way to remember those long dead and the fact that "War is Hell"!

For me, trying to finish "JUST BEFORE TAPS" could be "a race against time"." When I started this book in June 2014, I was eighty six years old, had major health issues, was nearly blind and had to try to type it on my computer using a magnifying glass so I could read what I was writing. My July eye surgery rectified that problem somewhat and I was able to go a little faster, at least as fast as my elderly mind, my single remaining eye, and my "one finger" typing style would allow.

I survived some pretty rough days; my eighty seventh birthday; a few trips to the Emergency Room and it looked like, at least for a while, things were going pretty well for me. But looks can be deceiving.

The results of recent blood work, done a few days ago, indicates my GFR (kidney function test) over the past months, has dropped from the mid 50s to 30, my BUN has risen from about 30 to the mid 50s and my Creatinine has risen to 2.1 from about 1.2. The rapidity of the change concerns me as it means that, along with my other problems, I am on the border of going from Stage Three to Stage Four renal failure. Not good! If the downward spiral continues at the current pace I may be hearing "Taps" before the book can be finished. I guess "hearing" in that case would be an oxymoron. I will continue to write as long as I can and pray that it will be long enough. But that decision is in the Hands of Someone far greater than I.

While numerous local volunteer groups provide thoughtful activities for us to enjoy the year around, their participation accelerates even more as Christmas draws near. They show the kindness, patriotism and concern that helps make our lives here, as seriously service disabled veterans, more bearable and we look forward to their coming with great anticipation. Today December 10th, was a very special day as Ladies Auxiliaries, from three different American Legion Posts came to see us, at Trinka Davis Veterans Village, bringing loads of gifts with them. They toted them into the

Fred Kelley Clubhouse, trip after trip, and arranged them by categories on large round tables that were loaded to the brim. Each resident was allowed to choose three gifts from a wide selection that included things like clock radios, house slippers, shirts, socks, pajamas, and so many other wonderful choices it is impossible for me to list them all. So much for us to see and so hard for us to choose, we had to be sure we picked just the right ones! We went from table to table and back again picking and prodding, checking sizes and trying to make up our minds. We must have looked like a bunch of oversized kids in a candy store! Hopefully, no one took our pictures!

These lovely ladies from the Auxiliaries were wonderful! There was President Jeannette Henderson and Member Patsy Welch from Post 143 in Carrollton; Donna McCain and her mother Mrs. McAnsh, from Post 145 in Douglasville; President Priscilla Woody from Post 264 in Mableton plus some others whose names (please forgive me) I missed. Troopers all, they had given unselfishly of their time and talent to see that we residents of Trinka Davis Veterans Village, CLC were not forgotten as this Christmas draws near. As one of the residents who is no longer able to go home to spend Christmas with my family, it brought a feeling of "belonging" and I am so grateful for their warmth and generosity. I watched the faces of the other residents as they made their gift choices and it was obvious they all felt as I did. Mere words alone are not sufficient to express our appreciation!

Not all is wine and roses if you reach the point in life where you require the care and assistance of a facility like Trinka Davis Veterans Village, CLC, just to keep on functioning and to reduce the pain you live with day after day. I have studiously avoided writing about the pain of separation from my family because telling about it is hard. Sometimes I wake up in the early morning and reach over to touch my wife of nearly fifty years before I realize she is no longer there. It leaves me with an empty feeling and brings tears to my eyes to have to face the fact that life as I knew it is over. The years of happiness I knew are gone, never to return again this side of Heaven. The things we were able to do as a couple that brought joy to our hearts is never going to happen anymore. This is very difficult to live with and you do your best each day to shove those feelings to the back of your mind. Not an easy thing to do!

The only thing that eases the kind of pain I have described are the frequent visits from my family to let me know I am still important in their lives, the understanding attitude of the staff as they care for my aches and pains, and the coming of the many wonderful volunteers who unselfishly give so many hours just to spend time with us to let us know they care and that our sacrifices still have meaning. For me, Christmas Day will be especially difficult as I will spend it alone, seventy miles away from my family. This is the first time in nearly fifty years we will not be spending the Holiday season together and it is not a pleasant thought. Oh, my family will be coming to see me and we will have a kind of early Christmas together but it is not the same.

This morning at the breakfast table I looked around at the other C-House residents and quickly realized that I was not the only one who had lost many of the important things in life. W.J. lost his wife of over sixty years in 2005. L.B.'s family, that he had been counting on to take him home for Thanksgiving Dinner didn't bother to show up or call and yet, in his heart of hearts he hopes that they will not forget him again on Christmas Day. He is too good of a man to deserve that kind of treatment. There are several other examples of neglect I could recount but I will pass on those for now.

I guess, when you stand back and look at it, I am more fortunate than many of the residents at Trinka Davis Veterans Village. I have a very close family that continually shows me how much they care. Some of the other residents have no families left to care about them while a few others have families who only seem to care about what they can get for themselves out of their father's assets and his veterans compensation checks. Fortunately, these are in the minority. What partially fills the gaps in their empty lives and to some extent in mine, are the members of the staff and the many volunteers who help us get through the day and look forward toward another. If you are a seriously service disabled veteran and you need the kind of care that is given at Trinka Davis Veterans Village there is no place, and I mean no place, that does it better. What Trinka Davis and the Trinka Davis

Foundation did to help us service disabled veterans by constructing this "first of a kind" facility and donating it to the VA is a "Godsend"! Most of us who benefit from it will thank them as long as we live.

Every month we have a meeting of the Resident's Council in the Fred Kelley Clubhouse to get the skinny on what is taking place at Trinka Davis Veterans Village, CLC and today was the day. Several issues were raised including the sprinkler system and dangerous laundry room door that constantly assaults O.W. and myself. The promise of fixing the darn thing was repeated again. W.J. was visibly upset and beat his hands on the table espousing his belief that the lack of egress and ingress from inside to outside the facility and back was an infringement on freedom and his constitutional rights. I personally believe W.J.'s biggest concern really is egress and ingress through the fire door near his suite that provides him with unabated access to his bird feeders. If that problem could be solved I believe the rest of his rant might be a thing of the past. It was explained at the meeting that, due to the possibility of terror attacks on government buildings, access to Trinka Davis Veterans Village would be limited to only those who could furnish proper identification. Apparently, a resident covertly opening a locked door to go outside the building and back inside might provide an opportunity for someone with improper intentions to enter and do damage to the facility and/or the residents.

In a way this makes perfect sense. These are perilous

times! Terror attacks in the USA are not only possible but probable! Since government buildings filled with people, present a tempting target, this is a point that is hard to argue against. Could this happen to Trinka Davis Veterans Village in Carrollton, Georgia? Although it is possible, hopefully not. Can an exception be made to exclude this facility from a government regulation concerning security? Absolutely not! Can W.J.'s bird feeding problem be resolved? Sure! As I previously pointed out, we have a lot of large VA policemen on site and all are armed. Having one accompany W.J. through the fire door to the outside to feed his birds and back again might be the simplest answer. As big as these guys are they could even carry his bird seed bucket. In their left hand of course!

As the days fly by, Christmas is once again almost upon us. Today Saturday, December 13th, is bright and sunny and a bit warmer than usual for this late in the year. The day brought with it a 10:30 am event in the Fred Kelly Clubhouse which played to a packed audience. The "event" was a visit by several members of American Legion Post 294 in Powder Springs, Georgia who came bearing Christmas gifts for each of us. They were introduced to us by retired Chief Master Sergeant Fred Hilley and they circulated through the crowd swapping "war stories" with us. Since Powder Springs is about forty miles from Trinka Davis Veterans Village these guys must have gotten up with the chickens to make it here that early. And when we looked in our "packed solid" gift bags we were glad they did!

What our brother former service members had brought us were the kinds of things we really need! Baby powder, Colgate toothpaste, a quality toothbrush (for those of us who still have teeth) under arm deodorant, two pair of socks, a stocking cap (to keep our ears warm on those cold trips to Kroger's), a zipper change purse, and lots of sugar free candy for us diabetics. All these were topped off by an American flag which protruded above the "loaded to the brim" Christmassy bag the much appreciated treasures came in. We hit the jackpot! Thanks fellas! The time of their visit had been arranged with the assistance of our eminent Recreational Therapists Anthony Beard and Steve Duvalt, who sat in a corner with sheepish grins on their faces. I have a hunch that it was they who suggested the "sugar free" candy when they set the event up with our Post 294 American Legion brothers. Always looking out for our interests, aren't they? Yeah, sure!

I have been a resident of C-House in Trinka Davis Veterans Village, CLC, exactly seven months today. It is another cold Monday morning, at about 5:30 am, and I'm in my bathroom shaving when a knock comes at my door. A voice calls out something but, as I hadn't put my hearing aids in, I couldn't make out what was being said. I shouted back that I was indisposed and to come back later. They did - in force. As I sat on my bed in my bathrobe, CNA Heather Lewis jabbed my finger to get a drop of blood to check my blood sugar count while RN Ann Wyatt rolled up the sleeve on my right arm; tied a wide rubber band around my arm and drew two vials of blood for testing. Heather also left a bottle for a urine sample. What a way to greet the day! Both Ann and Heather are very nice ladies so I couldn't get too upset about the early morning assault on my dignity. Besides, Heather is pregnant and expecting around April 1st. FYI - it's a boy!

After getting dressed I went out to the breakfast table, wheeled my power chair into my usual spot which is next to W.J. The old curmudgeon hasn't been his usual pleasant self these days. He starts off every morning harping about supposed injustices in the shape of rules and regulations created by the Veterans Administration. After nosing around a little (I'm good at that) I discovered access to his bird feeders was not the problem. It seems he has already been offered help in this matter by sending someone outside with him to fill his feeders but, apparently, he wants to do it on his own.

I have reached the conclusion that W.J.'s real problem may be the loss of "independence" that always comes when you get to the point that you can no longer care for yourself and with age and serious service connected disabilities that happens more often than you might imagine. Entering a nursing home, even one as nice as Trinka Davis Veterans Village, CLC requires you to comply with their rules and regulations, most of which are actually created for the benefit of patient care. Is it hard? Certainly! Giving up your independence is one of the most difficult decisions you will ever make. But you make it because you no longer have a choice. You must give up the life you've always known because you simply cannot live it anymore. It is gone forever!

Often, this means being permanently separated by distance from the family you love; no longer being able to go when and where you want; loss of your ability to drive and oh so many of the everyday things you always took for granted. In W.J.'s case, he cannot seem to accept the loss of what he considers "his independence" so he verbally strikes out by blaming both rules and regulations as well as the very ones who are trying to help him most. Facing facts and accepting them for what they are apparently is difficult for some people. Sadly, there is nothing I can do about W.J.'s "problems" but try to keep on being his friend. And that I will do.

Today, Tuesday December 16th, was our last spiritual service, in the Trinka Davis Veterans Village Community Living Center's Chapel, for the year of 2014. Chaplain Jimmerson is still "part time" so we only have services in our Chapel every couple of weeks. Today was our "Christmas service" with stirring Carols and a sermon that was both typical for this time of year and well delivered. Our Chaplain, being a lady, had on an unusual set of dangling earrings with red bulbs that continually flashed on and off. My wife Jeanne who is a "dangly" type earring fanatic would go absolutely wild over these. I guess it is a "woman" thing.

While the service was great and the Chaplain is a "joy filled" person (if you get my meaning) I really miss the liturgical services we had at St. Clements. The Advent candles;

174

the Advent wreath and the Celebration of the Twelve Days of Christmas that begins on Christmas Eve and carries on all the way through to Epiphany on January 6th. While I am an Episcopalian, this is something Roman Catholics, Eastern Orthodox, Lutherans, and a few others who have liturgical type services will also understand. There are many ways of reaching out to God so who am I to judge the way different denominations do it. I think God accepts all who worship, love, and respect Him. I also believe He must have a superb sense of humor!

December 16th a fabulous Holiday Party was given for the residents by the staff and it was held in the evening at the Fred Kelley Clubhouse. The gala arrangement crew, consisting mostly of nurses and CNAs, was led by our eminent Social Worker, Jennifer Talley, who arrived in a stunning red dress in honor of the season. We were all seated around tables, staring at the decorations and the large lighted Christmas tree and impatiently waiting with expectant looks on our faces. I arrived a little early so I could find an appropriate spot in which to park my wheelchair where I wouldn't miss the action. I was almost struck dumb when I realized that someone with a weird sense of humor had fitted both H.Y. and H.C., from A-House with colorful Elf hats. H.Y.'s hat was "ears up" and H.C.'s hat was "ears down. For some unknown reason both seemed to look the part. Maybe it was the silly looks on their faces or maybe it was just my imagination.

175

The first order of the evening's business was the distribution of large sugar cookies, plunked on square plates, to each resident. Next came tubes of colored frosting and shakers with little colored sugar beads to decorate the cookies. L.B., who sat on my left, loaded his cookie with a messy heap of frosting; P.A., the rather large veteran, who sat directly across from me, did what he called a "tie dye", heaped high with frosting; while H.C., with the Elf hat, in his wheelchair on my right, streaked frosting from side to side and powdered it with the little colored beads. I made a pitiable resemblance to what I hoped looked like a multi colored Santa Claus and viewed my effort with pride. P.A. immediately gobbled his creation down and looked over toward mine. About that time, I had a "Lasix moment" so I had to make a potty call and, knowing P.A.'s prodigious appetite, ate my cookie to save it from the possibility of losing it in my absence.

Hot cider, in mugs was the drink of the evening. Much of it was delivered from table to table by the CLC Nurse Manager, Steven Releford, who, in his white medical smock, looked somewhat like a big, friendly teddy bear that had rolled in the snow. He also got stuck with the job of delivering plastic forks for the delicious lemon cake and bore all his assignments with a continual grin. Dr. Jamya Pittman, beautifully dressed in red under her white smock gave a speech that I couldn't hear over the noise. It must have been a humdinger as everybody applauded. She pitched in and helped while keeping an eagle eye on the residents. Especially the diabetics who, like me, are prone to over consumption when the opportunity arises. Nurse Practitioner Mrs. Marmom Warner, who wore a red sash over an off white blouse with black slacks, also helped while observing our gluttonizing conduct which I can, with tongue in cheek, absolutely assure her was appropriate. At least none of us got caught at it. Prizes for the best door decoration were given out to the winners of which C-House had none. As we all had to get back to our suites for "pill time" the party ended shortly after seven pm. It was a "whiz bang" while it lasted!

On December 17th, at about 11:30 am, my ordained Deacon, Judith Kalom and her husband, Peter arrived at Trinka Davis Veterans Village from St. Clements Episcopal Church in Canton to visit and provide me with Holy Communion. This was the fourth trip they have made to see me in the seven months I have been a resident here. The round trip distance they have to drive just to get here and return is about one hundred and forty miles. While we have services in the TDVV Chapel every couple of weeks there is nothing that lifts you so much spiritually as a visit from a member of the clergy and/or church members from your home church. Lay Eucharistic Visitors also frequently visit and take Holy Communion to my wife Jeanne at her Assisted Living residence in Canton. It is heartwarming to know that when you can no longer participate in Sunday services, due to age and disability, you have not been forgotten. Thank you Father Jamie for leading a church that cares! Words cannot describe the warmth I feel!

Christmas Day is just a week from today! There is both great happiness and some hidden sadness among the residents of C-House. Great happiness from those who are going to be able to spend Christmas at home with family and hidden sadness among those of us who either have no family to visit or those who, like me, are no longer physically able leave the facility. In either case it is hard to deal with and it leaves you with an empty feeling in your gut! I am more fortunate than some because my family will be visiting me on Sunday, December 21st and although it is not the same, we will celebrate the Holiday a few days early. I can live with that! In addition, the empty feeling of "loss" is somewhat reduced by the numerous visitors and organizations who come here almost daily to leave small gifts and wish us a "Merry Christmas"! Their continual presence here enriches our changed living situation far more than they might realize! Thank you volunteers!

This is Saturday, December 20th. The ice cream and cookie folks, better known to us (and the nation) as the Patriot Guard Riders (PGR) of Georgia, are due any minute. They come here faithfully, at one pm, every third Saturday of the month and are eagerly welcomed to the Fred Kelley Clubhouse by residents who usually try to beat them there to get a delicious bowl of ice cream (or two) and a mouth full of tasty sugar wafers. Members of the Georgia Patriot Guard Riders of Georgia are officially registered members of the

Patriot Guard Riders national organization. Their main mission is to attend the funeral services of fallen American heroes as invited guests of the family. The missions they undertake have two basic objectives. First, to show their sincere respect for our fallen heroes, their families, and their communities, and, second, to shield the mourning family, and their friends, from interruptions created by any protestor or group of protesters by strictly legal and non-violent means. Many of the members ride motorcycles and use them to protect the family from the view of protesters and to drown out their unwanted vocal protests with the sound of their "revved up" motorcycle engines.

Their fearless leader, Jerry Green (aka "Crawdaddy"), is both a veteran and a longtime member of the Patriot Guard Riders. He heads up this crew of ice cream dippers and sugar wafer distributors (including his grandson, Aidyn) in liberally doling out the treats. Butter pecan was today's favorite with the ice cream addicts. Chocolate ran a very close second. Jerry informed me that Georgia Riders carry the American flag in their left hand...leaving the right free to salute the fallen hero. He also explained how the Patriot Guard Riders in Georgia assist military veterans through an organization called "Help on the Homefront" or HOTH. Among its worthy purposes is to actively visit Veterans Administration hospitals and homes throughout the State of Georgia and to establish long term relationships between members and Veterans to support the quality of life needs of Veterans and their families.

As I am both a diabetic and an ice cream fanatic, I left a few minutes early. I am totally unable to control my desire for "seconds"! After the event was over Jerry and his grandson Aidyn, came over to my suite to bring me a Christmas card and a beautiful Georgia Patriot Guard Rider coin which I will treasure. See you in January, 2015, Jerry! Next time bring plenty of butter pecan!

They are here! The happy thought raced through my mind as I watched my wife, our daughter Julie, my son-in-law Tom, and my grandsons Neil and Cory come through the double doors of C-House. I had been parked in my wheelchair in the foyer near the big stone fireplace anxiously awaiting their arrival. They entered the foyer and came over to where I was sitting, exchanging hugs and kisses, and loaded down with gifts. We went back to my suite and they plunked them down, one by one until my bed was covered with packages tied with gaily colored ribbons! Since I was no longer physically capable of making the seventy mile trip to Canton for our annual Holiday gathering, Sunday, December 21st was the day we had chosen to celebrate an early Christmas together at Trinka Davis Veterans Village. And celebrate it we did!

The first order of business prior to opening the multitude of gifts they had brought me, was lunch at Ruby Tuesday's in Carrollton. Navigating the distance between C-House and Julie's Toyota through the long halls was difficult for me but a little strategy solved the problem. I rode my power chair to Fred Kelley Clubhouse while Jeanne pushed

180

my rolling walker. I parked my vehicle in a vacant corner, transferred to my walker and proceeded down the sand colored brick walkway to the turn area where Tom waited in Julie's car. My grandson Cory, took my walker to the trunk while the others helped me into the passenger side of the front seat. Since there wasn't seating room for all of us in Julie's car, Neil had driven his fancy hard top, girl attracting BMW convertible. He and Cory (both single) plopped their backsides into it and we all caravanned to Ruby Tuesday's.

When we arrived at our destination, we quickly discovered the "church crowd" had beaten us to the eatery and the place was packed! We were unable to get a table large enough to seat all of us so we settled for two "back to back" booths. The meal was absolutely delicious. Jeanne and I shared a booth with Tom and Julie while the boys took one together. Jeanne, Julie and I had a petite sirloin with coconut shrimp; Tom got his usual salmon; Neil chose a rib eye and Cory ate huge hamburgers. The loaded salad bar came with the meals and, as usual, it was great. On the way back to Trinka Davis Veterans Village we stopped at a Dollar General so I could get the things I needed plus three bags of cat treats for Snoopy's Christmas. Boy - that cat can eat! When we got back to TDVV we unloaded. I took my walker down the brick sidewalk and retrieved my power chair from where I had parked it for the trip back to C-House. There is more than one way to skin a cat (sorry Snoopy!) when you need to figure out how to overcome your disabilities to get where you want to go.

When we returned to my suite I opened the mound of presents on my bed. They were just what I needed. A new soft, fluffy bathrobe, a heated throw to keep me warm, books to read, a large container of diverse nuts from Neil, and a "Piggy Pack" containing summer sausage and cheddar cheese from Cory. In turn, I gave my wife, Jeanne, a pair of dangling diamond ear rings that had the words "I Love You" engraved on the back sides to match the "I Love You" engravings on the backs of the pendants I earlier presented to my daughters Julie and Sandy. I got a warm kiss from Jeanne as a reward. Just because we are a bit older doesn't mean the love and romance has gone out of our long marriage. Actually, it increases day after day. Now all my girls will forever know just how much I love them. And that is a lot! All in all, it was a great Christmas for me, even if I couldn't share it with them at home on the actual day. A few days early but still great! There is nothing like family!

The visit from my family wasn't the only event that took place on December 21st. There was another and, for those involved, very important. My C-House neighbor, C.B., celebrated his eighty ninth birthday with a rocking party in the Fred Kelley Clubhouse from two to four pm. The place was jammed to the walls with C.B.'s family plus numerous Trinka Davis Veterans Village, CLC residents. While I missed it, because the timing coincided with the hours I was sharing an early Christmas with my family, I did get to witness a little of it when I returned from Ruby Tuesday's to pick up my power chair from the corner of the Clubhouse. I noticed, with studied interest, the bountiful supply of ice cream and cake, and, although it was tempting, I couldn't partake because Julie had also brought ice cream and chocolate pecan pie to cap off our early Christmas celebration. To have stuffed myself at both C.B.'s Birthday party and Julie's pie and ice cream Social would have brought another shot of insulin in the belly. No thanks! Been there...done that!

T'was the "Day Before Christmas" and all through C-House residents W.J., O.W., C.B., and J.M. were preparing go home to share Christmas with their family. Lucky devils! That leaves just six of us here to hold down the fort and enjoy the Christmas dinner that is being served in the Fred Kelley Clubhouse to residents of "A", "B", and "C" Houses who, for one reason or another must spend their Christmas day here in Trinka Davis Veterans Village, CLC. For some of us "stay behinds" (like me) the reasons are physical. Others either have no family to spend Christmas with or have family members that don't care about anything beyond grabbing the service disabled veteran's compensation money for themselves much less spending Christmas with the one they take it from. Those are the "ingrates" and Thank God they are few. I am fortunate in that my family made a trip of a hundred and forty traffic filled miles just to share an early Christmas with me this past Sunday. I thank God everyday for my wonderful, caring, family! My heart aches for those veterans living here who do not have what I have.

It is quiet here as the afternoon before Christmas passes into evening, in C-House. There are no "stockings hung by the "chimney with care" and no expectations of a visit from "Santa Claus"." The jolly old gentleman has already made his rounds at Trinka Davis Veterans Village in the form of the numerous volunteer groups that came to cheer us up and bring presents galore! We were not forgotten! As evening passes into night we who remain will snuggle down into our beds and dream dreams of what once was while silently awaiting the dawning of Christmas Morning! Well maybe not so silently. Possibly a snore and even a tear or two!

I awoke Christmas Morning, about five fifteen am and looked at my ceramic Christmas tree to see if by some off chance Santa had made another trip to C-House to leave a little something extra. Seeing nothing bedside the tree, I glanced at my bedside table where I had left some little Hershey bars for the jolly old elf but they sat there untouched. I performed my morning ablutions, dressed, and headed outside my suite toward the kitchen to see if the coffee was ready. My way was blocked by the large scales that CNA Jamal had parked in front of my door to catch me for my morning weigh in. After my vitals were taken, and my finger punched to check my blood sugar, Jamal brought me several large packages that had been left under the big Christmas tree in the C-House foyer. A label bearing my name was attached. Wow! The jolly old elf, represented by a group of "Santa's Helpers" from an organization called "Soldier's Angels", had made it after all. And what a treasure trove of gifts they had brought with them! CNA Jamal Robinson put it all on my bed to be opened after breakfast.

Heading out to check the indicator on the coffee pot to see if the light was green, I noticed L.B. sitting in a chair next to the side wall with a dejected look on his face. I wheeled over to where he was perched and told him of my good fortunate. I informed him of Santa's visit and let him know that presents for everybody had been left under the tree. Jamal Robinson went to get those that had been left for L.B. When he handed them to him, L.B's eyes lit up, his mood changed instantly and a wide smile came across his face. He had not been forgotten after all! L.B.'s Christmas had been saved by "Soldier's Angels"! He began to open his gifts on the spot and, as he examined each one, his smile grew even wider!

After breakfast, I returned to my suite and began to open my presents. While the gifts were impressive and welcome, what really impressed me was a Christmas card from the Medeiros Family of Fall River, MA, and a drawing of Santa with his bag of toys placed on a sheet of paper that had been colored by a child. It bore the words "Keep up the good work Hero! and "Merry Christmas"." It said "Thank You" and was signed "Jay Anna" in a childish scrawl. I was deeply touched! Also enclosed was a bookmark, with the heading bearing the words "May No Soldier Go Unloved" and explaining the wonderful mission of "Soldier's Angels"." Oh, yes! In addition to the other gifts, there was a beautiful, patriotic blanket with a tag stating "This blanket was made with love by Wanda Blackwell" plus the words, "BAE Systems, Greenlawn, NY", "Soldier's Angels"." I wish they could know what their act of kindness did for my friend, L.B. It saved his Christmas!

Christmas dinner was served a few minutes after noon in the Fred Kelley Clubhouse. It consisted of a wide variety of entrees plus trays of excellent deviled eggs and raw vegetables. I had prime rib with mashed potatoes and corn bread dressing while others chose either turkey or ham as their main course. The deserts included pies, cakes, and, my favorite, banana pudding. J.M., who had gone to Atlanta to spend Christmas, returned because something didn't work out and ate his Christmas dinner with L.B. and I. Sometimes the best laid plans.....! After dinner, I returned to my suite to rest and digest. I did. The rest of Christmas day was uneventful but a great time was had by all!

C-House has two regrettable losses in Staff recently. Both were for different reasons. The first loss was RN Lisa Leonhardt who resigned to take a position at Tanner Medical Center, in Carrollton. She is a great nurse and we will miss her. Tanner's gain is our loss and we wish her great success.

The second loss was tragic. RN Arletha Shanta Turner was killed along with her two youngest children on December 26, 2014. Her seventeen year old son who was driving, is at this time hospitalized in critical condition. The accident was the result of a "head on" collision on a two lane road. All the residents of C-House loved her as she was not only a great nurse but a very special person. She was the nurse who I called "My good luck charm" as she was with me at Atlanta VAMC that day in July when I had my unexpectedly successful eye surgery whose outcome enabled me to finish writing "JUST BEFORE TAPS"." She will be missed! C-House residents lost a friend! And Heaven gained an angel! See you soon Shanta!

CHAPTER TEN

It's a Brand New Year

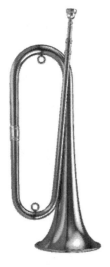

On New Year's Eve, the changeover from December 31, 2014 to January 1, 2015 arrived in C-House without fanfare at Trinka Davis Veterans Village Community Living Center. There were no horns or noise makers for the residents to blow or shake at the stroke of midnight. There were no exuberant parties where happy couples danced the night away, wore funny hats, drank champagne out of tall stemmed glasses and kissed each other heartily to welcome the New Year in as the clock slowly chimed out the Old. No, C-House residents had nothing much going on. Just a bunch of sleeping disabled veterans, snug in their beds, dreaming dreams of days gone by!

There were no New Year's Eve celebrations for the night nursing shift either. They were on duty standing watch over those sleeping disabled veterans ready if an emergency should arise and more than able to deal with it! RN Ann Wyatt was working hard at her desk in the nurse's office trying to catch up with the paper work. CNAs Morris Flowers and Latoya Vaughn were sitting in the living area eyes glued to the big TV over the white stone fireplace that was tuned to the

New Year's celebration waiting to see the annual Peach Drop in Atlanta. Both had their ears open wide for the possible sound of a call bell but, beyond that, all was quiet on the C-House front.

Morning also arrived uneventfully. I rose at five am; performed my usual morning duties and headed for the Laundry Room with a basket of dirty clothes which I stuffed into the washing machine. I threw in a couple of Tide pods, turned the machine on and managed to escape another assault from that nasty door. I checked to see if Morris had the coffee ready. The green light was on so I filled a mug, put in some creamer and returned with it to my quarters. Morris Flowers makes great coffee! He must have learned during his time in the Marines. I sat for a while, catching my breath and waiting for the pressure in my chest to abate, while watching the news. About six forty five am I peeked out my door to see if Mack (our Chef) had arrived. He had so I went to breakfast. Stomach full of Mack's great cooking, I picked up my finished laundry and returned to my room.

I rested until it was time for my morning bout of "Restorative Care"." Victor Ubani, MSN, the male nurse who is in charge of Restorative Care, was on vacation and his pretty CNA, Odinessa Spears, had the holiday off. Although one of them usually walks with me to make sure I do not overdo (fat chance of that) I decided I would walk by myself. I got my big rolling walker and slowly headed out my door to the hall. I took a right turn down the hall, walking carefully until that uncomfortable pressure feeling in my chest caused me to make my first stop. I plopped down in a chair near the locked double doors and across from the empty desk area to wait until the feeling eased. The next leg of my excursion took me to a bench across from the Police Office and the final portion to another empty desk/double door area where I rested for a while before reversing my journey. With appropriate stops, I returned to my suite. I have to try to keep walking so I can have the strength to go out to lunch when my family visits.

There are seventeen disabled veterans scattered among the three occupied Houses who are receiving Restorative Care. Some can go into the small exercise room and pump the stationary bicycle; lift small hand weights or work out on the treadmill. Others, like me, are pretty much limited to either bed and chair exercises or slow walking trips with the goal of maintaining as much strength and mobility as possible. It is a very important part of the overall care we receive as without continuing to exercise people fail much more quickly. Victor Ubani holds a Master's Degree in Nursing and like his capable Certified Nursing Assistant Mrs. Spears, has extensive experience in the field of Restorative Care. Together they make a great team and the residents under their care are better able to maintain an acceptable level of function which improves the quality of their lives.

There have been a couple of recent changes in the way LPNs and CNAs are assigned to the different Houses. Previously they were assigned to a specific House and stayed there permanently, except for "fill ins" when someone in one of the other "Houses" was sick or on vacation. That has been changed to a rotating status where LPNs and CNAs will spend three months in a "House" and then move on to spend the next three months in another. The "pro" of the new plan is that LPNs and CNAs get to know all of the residents and become familiar their various medical problems throughout the Community Living Center. The "con" is that, in my opinion, it breaks up the established relationships between staff and residents which allows instant knowledge of what to do when a serious problem arises. We will have to see how this works out. One plus in the plan is that the rotation does not apply to Registered Nurses who will stay in the "House" to which they have been assigned on a permanent basis. That should guarantee some continuity of care.

The other change affects W.J. and the bird feeding brouhaha. Since he and his door operating accomplice, (F.L.) were caught in the act by a VA police officer, W.J. has apparently decided to give up his "feed the birds by sneaking out the fire door" operation. The decision was made when his accomplice flatly refused to be involved in the scheme anymore. W.J. couldn't do the deed by himself without the danger of not being able to get back inside. Although he had been repeatedly offered staff help with his bird feeding, W.J. refused to accept it. So, according to him, the feeders are coming down and "bird fare" will now be a thing of the past. If he couldn't do the job by himself it just wouldn't happen.

191

W.J.'s "independence" was at stake. It is hard to understand his viewpoint as you come here to live because you need help and can no longer make it by yourself. Oh, well. Different strokes for different folks, I guess. In my opinion, it seems sort of like a case of cutting off your nose to spite your face or shooting yourself in the foot.

We just received some of our replacement CNAs plus two "day shift" LPNs from the management's newly designed "switch Houses every three months" revolving plan. Although I had been somewhat concerned about its effect on the residents, it turned even better than I thought it would. Teresa Easter, an excellent CNA who is also part Cherokee; will be in C-House for the next three months. So will LPNs John Corn and Kimberly Chambers, both of whom are thoroughly experienced and completely familiar with the medical problems of C-House residents. Kimberly is one of W.J.'s favorite nurses and John Corn is one of mine.

In addition, we picked up a lovely CNA Janice Lee, who has experience in Home Health Care, worked in a retirement home and took care of her dad who also was a veteran. While Janice currently lives in nearby Carrollton, she was born in Savannah and grew up infused with those courtly Southern manners. Janice plans on going back to college to obtain her RN Degree. Of African American heritage, she is a great fit for C-House and brings us "a touch of fresh air" that matches her friendly smile. Score four wins for C-House! We also have two replacement RNs who will take the place of RN Lisa

Leonhardt, who resigned to take a position at Tanner Medical Center and Arletha Shanta Turner, whose untimely death in an automobile accident greatly saddened us all.

Alternating on the rotating "night shift" with RN Ann Wyatt, to replace Mrs. Turner is Sonya Caldwell, RN, an attractive, rather petite, African American lady who is really not new to the CLC because she has filled in at the various "Houses" for several months. She is an excellent nurse and knows the residents and their various medical issues very well. Sonya has her BSN from the University of West Georgia and is a service disabled Army veteran who served in Europe. She lives in nearby Douglas County, is married with two children and comes from a family that has a long history of involvement in nursing careers and the medical field in general.

Prior to receiving her RN, Mrs. Caldwell started as a CNA at the VA Medical Center in Fayetteville, North Carolina where she was born. Her next step up the ladder was to become a surgical technician where she spent 15 years working in various facilities and operating rooms. She went on to earn her RN and became an operating room nurse. Sonya eventually came to Trinka Davis Veterans Village because it gave her the opportunity to serve her fellow veterans and to be close to her home. She is grateful for the great benefits the VA provides and plans on obtaining a Master's Degree so she can either teach nursing or become involved in case management.

On the "day shift" to replace Mrs. Leonhardt, is RN Rhonda Williams who has a total of 25 years of experience with the VA, including 10 years as an LPN, prior to earning her RN Degree from Lawson State Community College in Birmingham, Alabama. Born in Bessemer Alabama, Ms. Williams currently resides in Atlanta which gives her a 50 mile drive to get to Trinka Davis Veterans Village. She too is African American, and a "pleasingly plump" lady with a pleasant disposition and a wide smile. Ms. Williams says she came to Trinka Davis Veterans Village because she wanted to change to a new environment. She plans to continue her education on-line with the goal of receiving a Master's Degree with a focus on Nursing Management. Ms. Williams is getting married on August 29, 2015 to some very lucky fellow who hit the jackpot when she agreed to become his wife. With RN Sonya Caldwell and RN Rhonda Williams, score two more wins for C-House!

Saturday January 3rd was a remarkable day for me despite the constant light rain. My family (minus my two grandsons) came to visit and have lunch with me at the Olive Garden. Sandy and her husband Thomas Richard, made a four and a half hour drive, from their home north of Tallahassee, Florida; Julie, her husband Thomas Edward, and my sweet wife Jeanne traveled an hour and a half to get here from Canton, Georgia. It was the first time my family had been able to get together since I came to Trinka Davis Veterans Village and it was "catch up" time. Julie, Jeanne, and Thomas

Edward arrived about 11:45 A.M...arms loaded with a Christmas present that had been overlooked; three large bags of white cheddar cheese popcorn and three large jars of luscious baby dill pickles that I often share with my fellow pickle lovers, O.W., W.J., L.B., C.B., and J.G. Sharing food items purchased from the outside is something we do here. It is a military thing. Kind of like sharing the contents of a mess kit or a K ration in a foxhole, I guess. Sandy and Thomas Richard arrived about 12:45 P.M. and it was like old home week! Hugs all around and lots of "catch up" conversation. My heart was so "joy filled" I thought it would burst from the pleasure of seeing them all together again. Thomas Richard and Thomas Edward are both normally quiet guys, until they get together. From that point on they engage in constant conversation. They seem more like "brothers" than "brothers-in-law" and remarkably, even look alike. Julie and Sandy, even though they have different mothers, are both blondes. And the resemblance does not stop there! Both are intelligent, stately, self-assured, and beautiful. Both have happy long time marriages. No father could ask for better daughters. I have been truly blessed!

About 1:15 P.M. we got ready to leave for Olive Garden. I got into my power wheelchair while Jeanne pushed my large, rolling walker. When we got to the Fred Kelley Clubhouse I parked the wheelchair in a corner; transferred to the rolling walker and the six of us traveled up the wide sand colored brick walkway toward Julie and Thomas Edward's Toyota

Venza and Thomas Richard's and Sandy's big Ford extended cab truck. Julie put my walker in the trunk of her car. Both vehicles loaded, we headed out of Trinka Davis Veterans Village toward our destination, caravan style with the men doing the driving.

The meal at Olive Garden was excellent and the company even better. The two couples talked to each other endlessly while Jeanne and I proudly looked on. It was a "heartwarming" feeling to see them all together again and it is a memory I will carry to my grave. When lunch was over we returned to Trinka Davis Veterans Village, de-carred, went back down the sand colored brick walkway, past the Police Office and into the Fred Kelley Clubhouse ostensibly to retrieve my power chair. It didn't work out that way. A football game was playing on the big TV over the fireplace, so we sat down at a table so the boys (and girls) could watch the end of the Florida vs. East Carolina game. To everyone's joy, Florida won 28 to 20.

The game over, we returned to my suite to say our goodbyes. Julie had removed and packed the Christmas decorations she has so lovingly placed in my suite and gathered up a few items I had collected for my grandson Cory, plus several issues of the Blue Ridge, Georgia newspaper I had saved for Jeanne. That way, she would be able to catch up on the latest news from the lovely mountain area where we had spent a quarter century of our lives together. As my family prepared to leave my suite to return to their destinations hugs

196

and kisses were exchanged. Julie informed me that Emeritus Riverstone Assisted Living, where my wife, Jeanne and our crazy cat Snoopy, live, had recently been purchased by Brookdale and is now called Brookdale Assisted Living, Canton. Nothing much changed except the front door now has a "push button" opener which makes it easier for folks in wheelchairs to go in and out. Oh, yes. The monthly fee has been increased from $3120.00 to $3242.00. The increase seems like quite a bit for a door opener but Jeanne is well cared for and we can easily afford it. It is worth any price just to be assured of that. I was so happy because I had another chance to see them all together and kind of sad because you never know if this time will be the last time that will ever happen. I watched out the window and waved as they drove away.

I personally believe that VA Outpatient Clinics attached to Community Living Centers constructed in small cities like Carrollton, at least 40 miles from the nearest major VA Medical Center, represent the future of VA medicine. In a previous chapter, I promised to explain how other medical specialties are provided to Community Living Center residents and how they interlock to offer a range of services not readily available for seriously service disabled veterans who reside in private nursing homes at VA expense. The source of these medical specialties is our excellent attached VA Outpatient Clinic that not only serves thousands of area veterans but also the residents of our Community Living

Center.

The question seems to be how to accomplish something like this successfully without the usual long delays and huge cost overruns that too often come with construction efforts poorly planned and badly overseen by VA bureaucrats! There are plenty of examples. Orlando, VAMC for one. As a Master electrician, who worked on a number of large projects and as a seriously service disabled veteran who lives in such a facility, I have a suggestion. Why not follow the example set by Trinka Davis and the Foundation she created that was responsible for the fantastic job of constructing Trinka Davis Veterans Village!

That would require the use of tax exempt Foundations where patriotic citizens of means, who care about decent living conditions for seriously service disabled veterans, requiring long term care, could either individually or severally contribute funds toward such a purpose. The facilities could be constructed, on budget in a timely manner and donated to the VA upon completion. Certainly a "win win" situation for both the contributors the VA and the taxpayers!

Getting back to the subject of special medical services our attached Outpatient Clinic provides for both area veterans and CLC residents. I have personally been able to use several of those services myself. These include podiatric care, vision care, dental care, tele-medicine and radiology. The availability of these medical services within wheelchair range and under the same roof as the Community Living Center saves considerable money for the VA. It also saves CLC residents, many of whom are in failing health, from having to make some of those long, difficult, tiring, one hundred mile trips, often by ambulance or van, to Atlanta VAMC to obtain those very same services.

If some additional services such as orthopedics, dermatology, gastroenterology, a CT scanner, etc. could be added to the Outpatient Clinic in the near future it would, in addition to being cost effective, benefit both the area's thousands of veterans and the CLC residents and, at the same time, reduce a little of the patient overload at Atlanta VA Medical Center.

The Podiatrist is one of the first lines of defense and we formerly had one of the best and wittiest in Dr. Craig Murad, DPM, MBA. Unfortunately he was transferred to another VA facility in Nashville, Tennessee. Diabetics require frequent inspections of their feet ankles and lower legs and regular trimming of their toenails. I understand we will be getting a new podiatrist in the very near future. I hope his skill and sense of humor matches that of Dr. Murad.

Podiatric care is extremely important to diabetics like me because of the necessity of avoiding foot related complications. There are a number of diabetics in our facility. C-House alone has four of us who require regular care. Conditions like open sores on the feet are often slow to heal and bleeding corns and calluses require professional attention as do ingrown and fungal toenails. For diabetics, podiatric checkups are necessary to help in preventing the need for foot and lower leg amputations.

A while back, I thought I had broken a front tooth so I made an appointment with Dr. Elmo Newlin, DMD, at the Outpatient Dental Clinic to have him inspect the potential damage. While Dr. Newlin is the epitome of a "country dentist" he is actually a graduate of the School of Dentistry, at the Medical College of Georgia. He had worked on W.J., who is generally hard to satisfy, but who, in this case, gave me a glowing recommendation. He was correct. Dr. Newlin quickly discovered that the tooth in question was not broken, just a bit ragged from my constant tooth grinding. He did repair my upper partial plate by tightening it so it would stay in place. I join W.J. in recommending this fine dental professional. Besides, he is in close proximity to my suite and can be accessed quickly by power wheelchair in case of emergency.

We are fortunate to have both an Optometrist and an Optical Shop on the premises. The Optometrist is Dr. Shavon Bigoms, OD, a graduate of the Indiana School of Optometry. Since I was born in Indiana I was immediately prejudiced in her favor. We Hoosiers have to stick together She is not only an excellent Optometrist, she is also a very pleasant person. In today's world, Optometrists write prescriptions for necessary medicines and treat all kinds of eye diseases. If I live long enough and ever need a new pair of new glasses she will

200

be my first choice for the job. Her office is directly across from the Outpatient Clinic's Optical Shop operated by that skilled glasses fitter and frame bender, Mr. Eric Baly. He can help you pick out the proper frames, from his vast display, and make a wiggly pair of glasses fit so tightly they will no longer slip down your nose. Must be a trick to it. I could never do it! See you next time they slip, Eric!

We also have an Audiology Department for those veterans who need hearing aids due to damage from gunfire in the military which is most of us here. The examination is conducted by one Dr. McWhorter, an audiologist who knows the profession. The good doctor has a nice lady assistant who has repaired and adjusted my hearing aids several times and in one instance sent the right one back to the manufacturer for an overhaul. Sure works better. What was that you said? Oh, well.

The only other Outpatient Clinic service I have used to date, is tele-medicine also known as tele-health. I had a spot on my forehead that wouldn't heal and some kind of a lump in the lobe of my right ear that hurt when I touched it. Dr. Norvell, the head honcho at both Trinka Davis Veterans Village CLC and the attached Outpatient Clinic, sent me to said Clinic to have a couple of pictures taken of the areas and then sent by computer to the Dermatology Department at Atlanta VAMC. I went into a small room where a technician pressed some kind of camera first against my forehead and then against my ear and "snap-snap" the job was finished. It

201

turned out that the spot on my forehead was a basal cell carcinoma and the lump in my ear was a squamous cell cancer on my ear. How do they do that?

After another exam requiring a long trip to Atlanta VAMC Dermatology and a biopsy a doctor with a two and one half star rating located some distance from Trinka Davis Veterans Village was recommended by the VA to do the job at VA expense. No way! At my request, both cancers were eventually removed by Dr. David E. Schoenfeld, a five star rated doctor from Dermatology Specialists of West Georgia, right here in Carrollton and paid for with my Medicare and AARP supplement. The good doctor did a top notch job and the scars are almost invisible. Sometimes the VA is hard to understand.

The services offered at Trinka Davis Veterans Village Outpatient Clinic not only interlock with and help to expand the range of the medical and nursing care already provided for the residents of the Community Living Center, they also serve the thousands of veterans who live in this area. This saves many long trips to Atlanta VAMC to obtain "outpatient type" services that could, in my opinion, be performed locally and in a timelier manner. The recent legislation passed by Congress and signed by the President, allows for a substantial number of VA Outpatient Clinics to be built so it appears VA medicine is headed in that direction. My concern is that the "cost overruns" and "time delays" that frequently take place under VA supervision of construction may turn this plan into a "nightmare" for both veterans requiring care and taxpayers deserving a break! The example set by Trinka Davis and the Foundation she created, if utilized, could go a long way toward eliminating that situation. Construction would be on time and on budget! An impossible dream? I sure hope not!

There are three more "modalities" in use at Trinka Davis Veterans Village that provide great benefit to Community Living Center residents. Two are "therapeutic" and one is "protective"." I looked up the word "modalities" and used it in this instance because it seems to fit the situation. The "therapeutic" ones are "spiritual care" and "housekeeping"." I believe both are "cleaning agents"." "Spiritual care" cleans the soul through faith in a Higher Power and forgiveness of sins while "Housekeeping" cleans the facility by helping to eliminate unhealthy bacteria. To me, the two are somewhat alike as both provide for a better and healthier life.

"Spiritual care" at Trinka Davis Veterans Village is provided by Chaplain Monique Jimmerson whose major treatment room is the small Chapel located not far from C-House. Her "every other Tuesday services" are well attended by both African American and Caucasian veterans plus one (me) who has a sprinkling of Native American blood in his veins, courtesy of his maternal great grandmother. There is an old military saying "there are no atheists in foxholes" and it is pretty much on the mark. Veterans have seen it all and most are firm "believers"." Disabled veterans may be even more so as they have "seen the elephant" and know how tenuous life can be. Most of us, regardless of denomination, are regular "church goers"; read our bibles and/or prayer books regularly and thank God for His help and our existence. For us, "spiritual care" ranks high on our list as a successful treatment "modality"."

"Housekeeping" at Trinka Davis Veterans Village in both the CLC and the Outpatient Clinic is performed by an energetic crew of germ destroyers headed by Team Leader Kristin Franklin, also known as "Kristin the Ant Killer"." Her fight a while back against the dreaded sugar ants that had invaded C-House and the "lengths she went to, to win the battle" earned her a well-deserved promotion to a management position. Under her leadership, her crew successfully scours the entire facility (including our individual suites) every day to prevent germs that can cause illness and infections if allowed to go unchecked. Like "spiritual care", "housekeeping" is, in my opinion, also a valuable and important treatment "modality"!

The final "modality" on my list is what I call the "protective modality"." That is supplied by the twelve VA Police Officers who work alternating twelve hour shifts giving us twenty four hour a day protection against those who would do us wrong by committing crimes like theft of our belongings or try to illegally enter the Community Living Center without proper identification. These officers are well armed, well trained and except for their Sergeant, of a size and strength that would create envy in most NFL linebackers. In comparison, their Sergeant seems to be about the size of an average "place kicker" but the gun he carries in the holster on his right side makes him appear much bigger.

Because of recent demonstrations in various metropolitan areas where some of the demonstrators march and yell "Kill the Cops" I have deliberately omitted their names. It seems that those who encourage unstable individuals to murder police officers do not care what color those officers are. Recently, in New York City, one such nut ambushed two police officers sitting in their cruiser. One officer was Hispanic and the other was Chinese. However, I believe our VA Police Officers are alert at all times and more than capable of taking care of themselves. I did suggest that we disabled veterans were competent to handle weapons, had a lot of experience in the field, and could take care of ourselves if called upon to do so. As residents are not permitted to have firearms in this federal facility, my suggestion went over like a "lead balloon"!

One reason for increased security here is the possibility of terrorist attacks on federal buildings. We did have a recent incident just before Christmas where two Caucasian individuals, accompanied by a member of the facility's management, came into our Community Living Center and distributed over two dozen cheap, unreadable six point print Bibles. They contained many errors. I still have the one that was given to me. They also brought candy canes and sticks, some unwrapped, ostensibly as Christmas gifts for the disabled veteran residents. One resident ate some of the candy, became very ill, and I was told his lips turned blue from cyanosis. All the candy was immediately picked up from the residents who had received it. Cyanosis is the appearance of blue or purple skin or mucous discolorations due to low levels of oxygen. There are some twenty six causes, only one of which is poison.

W.J. claimed he ate some of the candy in question and it caused him no problem whatsoever. Since the resident who ate it, prior to becoming sick, had numerous other medical problems, some of which could have caused cyanosis, the candy was probably harmless. We residents heard no more about the issue as we are not privy to updates. I can only assume the individuals must have us meant no harm. However, it did demonstrate how easily someone could come in here and, if they had questionable intentions, something bad could have happened. Fortunately, the resident in question recovered and there have been no further incidents to date. A tempest in a teapot? Probably. But security has sure tightened since then.

In Trinka Davis Veterans Village Community Living Center, there are residents and staff of several different colors and shades. Some even have a bit of Native American blood. All get along together like one big, happy family and there is absolutely no racial intolerance! That is not because of some government regulation or the need for "political correctness."

It is because all of the residents and many on the staff are either veterans or family members of veterans. There is something about serving in the military that makes one understand how nonsensical racial intolerance is.

In the military, you don't care if the person you are facing a dangerous situation with, or sharing a foxhole with just trying to stay alive, is white, black, brown, red, yellow, or sky blue pink. He/she is your brother/sister and you have each other's backs. That feeling carries over in a place like Trinka Davis Veterans Village, CLC, because we all have so much in common. We are "brothers" and "sisters" and we will stand up for each other whatever the cost! It may be hard for some uneducated "bigot" to understand our attitude of mutual acceptance but that "bigot" probably never spent one day serving his country, only himself. That said, I will put an end to this chapter and get on toward the completion of "JUST BEFORE TAPS"!

CHAPTER ELEVEN

Time Marches on

Time moves forward rapidly and sometimes almost unnoticed! It suddenly dawned on me that I had been a resident of Trinka Davis Veterans Village Community Living Center for eleven months. It came as a shock as in the ups and downs of daily living I had completely lost track of time. The Christmas Holidays had come and gone and the New Year of 2015 entered Trinka Davis Veterans Village quietly. Suddenly the action got underway! In late January I was hospitalized in the Atlanta VA Medical Center for two days. The improvement that had taken place in both the Emergency Room and the tenth floor of the Hospital since my prior hospitalization in August, 2012 amazed me! It was outstanding for the most part and it was obvious that things had changed dramatically! During my short hospital stay I had a heart catheterization. It was done with great care and a minimum of dye as my kidneys are rapidly failing. The doctors discovered that I have unstable angina and, with my approval, they decided to try to treat it medically rather than place stents in my 60 to 70 percent blocked coronary arteries.

After I got out of the hospital and returned to Trinka Davis Veterans Village I sent a three page e-mail to VA Secretary Bob McDonald telling him about the improvement in care at Atlanta VA Medical Center. I also told him about a young physician, Dr. Roberto Brown, a Morehouse graduate who had impressed me with his knowledge, attitude and compassion. Secretary McDonald e-mailed me back asking if he could share the e-mail I had sent him with Ms. Leslie Wiggins, Atlanta VA Medical Center's Director. Naturally I told him "Certainly"." I believe people who do a great job should be recognized for their work. Too often in the past they have gone unnoticed by those in charge. But not with Secretary McDonald!

Valentine's Day and St. Patrick's Day came and went and the season of Lent ended up in the glory of Easter. Since my physical condition has deteriorated considerably it is increasingly difficult for me to go outside of the facility. My entire family came to Trinka Davis to celebrate Easter with me. And what a day it was! Jeanne, Julie, Thomas Edward, Neil, and Cory came from Canton loaded with food and Easter goodies. Sandy and Thomas Richard came from Tallahassee also loaded with food items. The Fred Kelley Clubhouse had been blocked off due to construction so Dr. Connie Hampton DNP, graciously allowed us to use the Celebration Room for our family get together. It has a long table with lots of chairs and an attached kitchen. The food was great. The company was greater and the day was one made for memories. It made me a happy man! I will never forget it.

I have really come to appreciate our Nurse Associate Manager, Dr. Connie Hampton, DNP. She is an intelligent and engaging individual who is always smiling and who interacts very well with the residents. She, along with the Physician Manager, Dr. Robert Norvell, M.D., an excellent Board Certified Internist, are responsible for overseeing and managing the entire operation at the Trinka Davis Veterans Village facility. This is not an easy job as the way our facility is set up it has to depend on Atlanta VAMC (some fifty miles away) for a lot of things including resident's prescription medications. This causes problems when medications that have been prescribed for residents are not available for the nurses to dispense. This has happened to me personally several times.

Fortunately, the drugs that were missing were not those I need to control unstable angina. From my discussions with other residents I discovered I am not the only one here this has happened to. Mistakes of this nature could result in serious problems and even cost lives if critical medications are not available to dispense when needed! This is not the fault of the RN's and LPN's who dispense the medications. You cannot give out medicines you haven't received. The problem obviously is that either the necessary medications were not ordered by the responsible individual at Trinka Davis or that they were ordered but not shipped from Atlanta. Personally, I believe it is probably the latter. In my opinion, an on-site pharmacy at Trinka Davis Veterans Village is badly needed. It could serve both the Outpatient Clinic and the Community Living Center and provide necessary medications to Outpatient Clinic patients and Community Living Center residents without delay.

It is extremely difficult to operate a large facility like Trinka Davis Veterans Village efficiently when the authority to make even minor decisions is divided between those who at the site of the problems and those who are fifty miles away from said problems. More autonomy for management locally could prove helpful providing periodic oversight from top management at Atlanta VAMC is in place and used in a reasonable manner. It is easier to arrive at a solution for a problem you can see than it is for one you can't!

Sometimes the news you get is not exactly what you want to hear. This is what happened to me in late April when my Nurse Practitioner, Mrs. Warner, brought me the results of my latest blood test. My GFR (measure of kidney function) has dropped to 27 which puts me firmly at Stage Four Kidney failure. My GFR has been dropping at the rate of about three points per month and a drop of twelve more points will put me in Stage Five which is the beginning of the "End Stage"." Since I am not going to take dialysis time is getting rather short for me. I understand that as kidney failure gets really bad it can result in confusion, dementia, and even hallucinations. I guess I had better write fast while my brain still functions. Or at least I think it does.

There have a lot of changes at Trinka Davis Veterans Village since I first rolled my carcass through its front doors on May 15, 2014. Some have been good and some maybe not quite so good. One of the pluses is the fact that we now have six Chefs to cook our meals for the three Houses currently in operation. For a while after my arrival CNAs and even the RNs were often stuck with the job of cooking breakfast in C-House. Since some of those good folks are still here I will not comment further. A minus is in the quality and variety of the food. A lot of it is prepackaged or processed and not good for residents with diabetes and/or kidney failure. While bringing the extra Chefs on board was an improvement the battle to improve the menu led by our dietitian, Kwanda McLemore, R.D., was a major victory. She and some of the others have designed a daily menu that permits residents to select what they want to eat from among the items listed.

The menu also lists what kind of a diet the resident is supposed to be on. This is one of the kinks in our new dietary system that hasn't completely been worked out yet. The residents are not told what they can eat. They are allowed to choose what they want to eat. Most do! And therein lays the problem, at least for me. Mine is a "Carb Controlled Renal Diet" and trying to figure out what I can eat to prevent my condition from getting worse has been a nightmare! Excessive carbohydrates are bad for my diabetes and excessive protein is bad for my failing kidneys. The menu offerings contain an abundance of both. I also am supposed to avoid (or consume in small amounts) foods containing potassium, sodium, and phosphorus so that doesn't leave me with much of a choice. Our friendly and capable dietician, Kwanda McLemore is searching hard for a solution to the problem and I know if one is available she will find it. She is tops at her job!

A couple of weeks ago the Staff moved everybody in C-House to D-House while they did some work on the sprinkler system. I got a suite with a view of a little field of dead grass and a wall. I kept the blinds down most of the time as I didn't enjoy looking out the window at the ugly sight. As one room had been converted into some kind of a calming room with music and tube lights that bubbled along with some comfortable chairs we were one room short.

My C-House next door neighbor C.B. drew the lucky straw and got to sleep in B-House for the two weeks we were there. For most of us it was an uncomfortable time. As the days went by most of us ran out of something but since C-House had been blocked off we had to do without. L.B. ran out of soap to do his laundry and conned one of my last pods. Old L.B. is pretty good at that. He is always out of stamps and while he borrows them frequently he never buys any or returns the ones he borrows. Since he is such a good guy nobody minds too much. He is raising watermelons this year and has promised me one. I am going to hold him to it!

When I first came here on May 15, 2014 only two houses were full. Each House had sufficient Staff on each shift consisting of an RN, an LPN, and two CNAs. All were well trained and the care was superb. Over the past year that has changed. We have a "Staff shortage"." We now have three Houses full of residents and the fourth and last is expected to open soon. I have seen times, especially at night, when one RN was trying to cover all three Houses by herself leaving only a LPN and a CNA to cover the individual Houses. Don't get me wrong. These are hardworking folks and they "make do"." But for some reason we are losing good people and not replacing them fast enough or with properly trained CNAs. I believe that Trinka Davis Veterans Village is a microcosm of the VA system and what is happening here is probably happening at other facilities. Something needs to be done!

W.J. was as unhappy as I was about our temporary move to D-House. His bird feeders went unfilled and he worried about his feathered friends. When he returned to C-House he had to clean out all his bird feeders as the seed had hardened from the rain. Somehow he still gets out the fire door to feed his birds. I think the Staff has given up trying to stop him and just turns a blind eye. One of the reporters on a local paper is a friend of his and a story is probably the last thing the VA out here wants. After all, W.J. will be 96 next month. While he has slipped some physically he is still sharp as a tack. When we got back to C-House on May 11th everybody heaved a sigh of relief. This two weeks it is A-House's turn in the D-House barrel. After that it will begin to fill up with new residents and the Community Living Center will soon be full.

Today is May 15, 2015 and it marks one year to the day since I became a resident of Trinka Davis Veterans Village! I celebrated by eating a Bun candy bar from a box of twenty four that I had shipped to me from Amazon.com. I began to eat them when I was a tot in Indiana and resumed the habit later when Jeanne and I made trips to the town of Garrett to visit my mother and my Aunt Fleta. They were a local product and they are delicious! Chocolate with peanuts and maple cream filling. Umm! I didn't realize they still made them until I ran across the fact while searching on Amazon. Thirty dollars for a box of twenty four! I used to buy them for a nickel a piece some eighty years ago and they had increased in price to a quarter back in the 1960's and 1970's! Now they are a buck and a quarter. I think my next box will be vanilla cream!

Shortly before my January hospitalization I lost a good friend and fellow resident. F.B. was in his nineties; retired Air Force and had served with the Tuskegee Airmen as a flight mechanic during World War II. When the planes returned damaged and shot full of holes it was his job to get them back in the air as soon as possible. F.B. was an African American who had joined the Army Air Force when the military was segregated and the policy still rankled him. We became unlikely friends when we discovered we were both long time Masons. That made us "brothers" in a way that only Masons can understand. In addition, both F.B. and I had kidney failure. He had been on dialysis for a number of years. It was not something he enjoyed. My kidneys are also failing but I have opted out of dialysis. I have decided that quality of life is more important to me than length of life. F.B. had a real sense of humor. One of our "jokes" was I would introduce him to outsiders as "my brother"." It brought some weird looks at times because of the color difference. We almost split our sides laughing when one of the people I informed that F.B. was "my brother" looked at us up and down and said in all sincerity "did you guys have different mothers?" F.B. eventually decided to discontinue dialysis and passed away shortly thereafter. The Chaplain was looking for someone to pray at his Memorial Service here at Trinka Davis Veterans Village and apparently wasn't having much luck. Two had refused. That was hard to understand as F.B. was respected and well-liked by both men. J.R., a Vietnam veteran and our Council Chairman asked me to do the honors. He said the Chaplain had told him this was an "interfaith service" and the name "Jesus" could not be mentioned.

I knew immediately why the others had refused and hit the ceiling! Not only was F.B. a "Brother Mason", he was also a devout Christian. It was an insult to his memory! I went back to my suite and typed up a paper headed "NO MEMORIAL SERVICE FOR ME", explained what I had been told could not be said at F.B.'s service and that if the name: "Jesus" could not be used at my Memorial Service there would not be any. I then filed it with the nurse and requested that it be put in my Medical Records. When it was discovered what I had done the roof blew off! A call was made to Atlanta by

216

someone who shall be unnamed and the prohibition against using the name of "Jesus" was immediately reversed.

I then agreed to do the prayer honoring F.B. and started it by crossing myself and beginning with the words "In the Name of the Father, and the Son, and the Holy Spirit"." As I spoke I could almost visualize my friend F.B. up in Heaven looking down, shaking his fist and saying "You tell 'em boy!" I also discovered afterward that a lot of people here agreed with my position. I have no idea who told the Chaplain to eliminate the name "Jesus" from the service but I sincerely doubt that it was her idea. I do have a hunch it will not happen again at Trinka Davis Veterans Village.

Every third Saturday of the month the Patriot Guard Riders (PGR) come in force bringing sugar free ice cream that tastes like the real thing! They started coming to Trinka Davis about a year ago to give back to our veterans. The event is called "The Lou "Soretoe" Costello Memorial Ice Cream Social" and honors one of PGR's finest leaders. The volunteers are headed up by Jerry "Crawdaddy" Green and "Soretoe's" widow, Carol "Twinkletoes" Costello. It's part of a program called *Help on the Homefront* (HOTH). While they may have strange ride names like Crawdaddy; Twinkletoes; KOP (Keeper of the Peace); JayDub; Quill; Chief Pappy; Red Mollie; JT; Sharpshooter; Gator, Knobby; Mack the Marine; Bud (our oldest PGR member and Korean War vet) and the Nettles, they have one thing in common, an unwavering respect for those who risk their lives for America's freedom and security. When they show up, they are met by a swarm of residents from "A", "B", and "C" Houses with canes, on walkers and with wheelchairs (both manual and power) ready, willing, and able to get down to the business of putting away as much ice cream as they could hold. Butter pecan is always the odds on favorite among the residents with chocolate running a distant second and vanilla bringing up the rear. Naturally my favorite is butter pecan and I am good for at least two bowls at a setting. Plus several sugar wafers of diverse colors. Ice cream is one of the few food items that holds much interest for me these days as my appetite disappears a little more with every point my GFR drops.

Today is the day the Patriot Guard Riders come to visit and I am looking forward to the fellowship they bring and, of course, the butter pecan ice cream. I have been so impressed with their mission that I have asked them to be at my Committal Service which will take place at Georgia National Cemetery in Canton. My daughter Julie has Ron "Chief Pappy" Papaleoni's phone number and will contact him when my time comes. I have made a special request and he has agreed to carry it out for me. I am being cremated and having my ashes dumped in a hole in my gravesite. He has agreed to put a half gallon of that delicious butter pecan on top of my grave and let it soak through. What a way to go! I will be watching you from above Chief! Don't try to get away with a pint!

Being buried in a National Cemetery is something I

have always planned on. My wife Jeanne, intends to be cremated also and she can be put in the same grave with me. I get the front of the tombstone to have my name and service engraved on and she gets the backside. We have been together a long time in life and want to be together for Eternity. That says a lot about a good marriage. And ours has been great! A real love match from start to finish!

I have no idea as to exactly when my time will come but have a strong feeling that it won't be much longer. I am surprised that I have managed to live as long as I have. When I look back and see that seventeen year old "wet behind the ears" boy that joined the Navy in 1944 and then look slowly forward and view all the events that took place as my life unfolded I can hardly believe it. Some of what happened to me during my long life is recorded in the first two chapters of my book "JUST BEFORE TAPS" and some elsewhere in various chapters as the book moves toward its climax. More can be found in the insert entitled "ABOUT THE AUTHOR"." My life has been full of the unexpected events that often took place in a surprising manner. One happened just today as I was eating butter pecan ice cream with the Patriot Guard Riders of Georgia and talking with Chief Pappy.

As my kidneys had been failing rapidly and time was getting short I had been wondering what was going to happen to the book I had laboriously written . . ."JUST BEFORE TAPS"." Since I am in no condition to go on with attempts to find a quality publisher I was at my wits end. Last month I had e-mailed the manuscript to Ron "Chief Pappy" Papaleoni who had indicated he would like to read it. I thought no more of it until I saw him today. I asked him what he thought. He told me he had sent a couple of chapters to someone who read it and was connected with the publishing business. And now the party wanted to see more of it.

Suddenly I realized what I wanted to do with my book. I had intended to give any proceeds to a top notch charity and the Patriot Guard Riders of Georgia sure fit the bill. What they do for veterans and their families is nothing short of amazing! I decided I would sign over all my rights to "JUST BEFORE TAPS" to their non-profit organization and they could do with it as they thought best. I personally believe the story would make a good movie. And maybe...just maybe...that is why it was written in the first place! Strange and unusual things happen now and then. At least to me. Kind of like being directed by some Grand Universal Architect?

With my belly stuffed full of butter pecan ice cream I headed back to my suite. I had polished off three bowls! A record for me. Usually I quit at two. But today seemed like a special day. I had found a solution to a problem that had been worrying me for quite a while. I was dying and time was getting short. What was I to do with the book I had written? Problem solved! And now I was at peace with myself. By the way, Chief Pappy is also a brother Mason.

Well, dear readers, the story of what happens in Trinka Davis Veterans Village has been told to the best of my ability in JUST BEFORE TAPS. It has covered the lives and service of a number of the residents who live here, it tells about the excellent Staff who works hard to see that we are properly cared for, and the wonderful volunteer organizations that make our lives more livable It even introduces the reader to "Jerri" the sweet lady barber who comes every three weeks to cut our hair without charge. It told about the attached Outpatient Clinic that serves thousands of area veterans. All in all a wonderful place that serves its severely service disabled war veterans very well. It is a credit to the VA!

The story of Trinka Davis Veterans Village, what it does for seriously service disabled veterans, and why it is known far and wide as the "Ritz Carlton" of Veterans Administration Community Living Centers has been told with all its wondrous advantages which far outweigh its few faults. It is the best the VA has anywhere in the US and more of them need to be built to serve those who became seriously disabled while serving our nation.

I have tried to tell the story with humor where indicated and to refrain from concealing the pathos which is the cost of war. The next stop is the Epilogue which ends the book by making some suggestions to improve the next facility like this one, a few probably unappreciated criticisms, and a couple of belly laughs. That will wind up what happens to each resident at our facility. . . JUST BEFORE TAPS.

Incidentally, the National Cemetery is my next stop where the bugle will give out its mournful sounds, for me.

Goodbye and God Bless! I have had a great life!

AFTERWARD

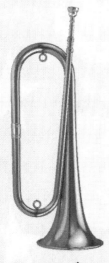

Trinka Davis Veterans Village came into being as a result of a strong desire by Trinka Davis to do something outstanding to help veterans. Although she did not live to see her dream fulfilled it was brought into reality by members of the Foundation she created and funded. No other VA nursing facility anywhere, throughout the whole United States, can compare to it or offer the quality of life to seriously service disabled veterans that it does. Not a single one! It was built on schedule and on budget by those who had the foresight to understand disabled veterans who had been seriously injured in the military sometimes require long term care, medical assistance, and interesting daily activities to give meaning to the lives they could no longer have. Did they succeed? You can bet your boots they did! Do the veterans who live there appreciate what was done for them? Absolutely! Could some minor changes help to improve a similar facility if we are fortunate enough to eventually have more built like Trinka Davis Veterans Village? Certainly.

When you build a new home you try to make it "perfect" so it will meet all the foreseeable needs of its occupants. As a former Master Electrician, who owned two contracting firms and worked on numerous large projects, I can assure you that is not going to happen! You never really know everything you need in a home until you have lived in it for a while! The same is true of any facility, be it an apartment building; a hotel or a Community Living Center like the one in Trinka Davis Veterans Village.

Having lived here as a resident for a quite a while, I am going to stick my neck out and offer a few suggestions that I believe should be incorporated in the original construction should a similar facility like Trinka Davis Veterans Village be built for the purpose of providing both long term care for seriously service disabled veterans and an "Outpatient Clinic" that furnishes quality medical care to area veterans. I am also going to make suggestions as to some simple steps the Veterans Administration can take to make Trinka Davis Veterans Village, and any other future facility like it, more efficient and livable. This is not meant as a criticism of the Veterans Administration. Trinka Davis Veterans Village, with its Outpatient Clinic and an attached Community Living Center is probably a first for them too!

The interior double doors in the four Community Living Center "Houses" are a good place to start. They have been installed in such a way that ingress and egress is quite difficult for residents in wheelchairs. There are no push buttons installed that you can push to open them so a disabled person is able to go in and out with ease. You must drive your wheelchair, power or manual, up to a point where you are close enough to grab a door handle with one hand and pull to hold it open so you can get you and your wheelchair in or out. That leaves you trying to use your other hand to propel yourself through the door quickly before the darn thing shuts on you. If you think it is easy I will gladly loan you my power wheelchair so you can try to do it. It can be done but it takes a while to get the hang of it. My solution. Put the push button openers on the doors at the time the facility is built. Easier and cheaper than trying to do it afterward!

The same solution applies to the very heavy doors that allow ingress and egress to the small laundry room where the washer and dryer are located. The door opens into a not too wide hall and wheelchair availability is nearly impossible. To get in with my laundry I must use my rolling walker and pull open the heavy fire door with one hand while trying to get my walker and dirty clothes basket with the other. Getting back out is much worse and dangerous! Both O.W. and I have had our arms whacked four times when we were unable to get through with our walkers and clothes baskets quick enough. As we are both old and our skin tears and bruises easily this represents a real hazard for residents like us. Despite numerous promises from the staff to fix it nothing seems to ever get done. Push button openers installed inside and outside on the walls near the door during construction would easily solve this problem.

The final door problem involves the double doors that

provide access to this facility. All were originally installed without push buttons that would allow ingress and egress to the building. Eliminating push buttons on the Main Entrance doors is probably a good idea because those who enter the facility are required to pass a manned Police Office and if not known as residents or staff, identify themselves to a VA Policeman and sign a register. However the other access doors should have been installed, at time of construction, and provided with safety locking equipment that would allow entrance only to those who have been issued either non-reproducible keys or assigned a code in case the entry is keyless. I understand this is currently being done at Trinka Davis Veterans Village, CLC, by the VA in order to limit unauthorized access.

In addition, the access doors in question are rather flimsy, were installed with large glass panes and provide little or no protection against illegal entry. They are also directly across from, and in full view of unmanned desks which do nothing at all to correct the situation. At this time in our history, terror attacks on government buildings are a real possibility. Currently, terrorists could break through these doors in two minutes flat, be completely out of view of police protection, and wound or kill residents and staff members almost with impunity. I would hope that this situation is rectified at time of construction on future facilities like Trinka Davis Veterans Village.

I had a serious problem this morning. My blood

pressure shot up to 194, I had a pressure feeling in my chest and a tight band feeling around my head. I was in trouble! I pushed my call buzzer. The CNA came into my suite. I asked for a nitroglycerin tablet, which, when shoved under my tongue, stops the problem in minutes. My blood pressure drops, the chest pressure resolves itself and the tight band feeling around my head goes away. Problem solved!

Although I am "PRN" for nitroglycerin getting it, under current VA regulations, is another story altogether! In my case, the CNA called the LPN, who in turn, had to call the RN, who happened to be the only RN on duty covering all three Houses. By the time she arrived and finished questioning me nearly 20 minutes had elapsed! I have been promised this will not happen again but, based on past experience, I don't believe it. Due to VA regulations, and the probability that some other RN, not familiar with my problem, is on duty when it happens I am going to take this promise with a "grain of salt"! A big one! In cases like mine, where nitroglycerin is needed immediately, residents should be allowed to keep it in their nightstand drawer. The life it would save could be my own!

Unfortunately for me, my blood pressure did not stay down. Although nitroglycerin lowers it temporarily, it rose again to 193. Not good! Fortunately, for me Dr. Rivera arrived on schedule with my favorite German Shepherd, her Therapy Dog, Outlaw. They rode to my rescue and helped restore my feeling of calm. Their visit was reinforced by some clonidine, courtesy of Dr. Jamya Pittman, who came into my suite to check me over. Although I realize that my days on this old earth are drawing to a close, and I am completely at peace with that, for some reason the good doctor wants me to stick around a while longer. She and Nurse Practitioner Mrs. Warner, are doing their best to see that I do and, while I am flattered, I know in my gut that theirs is a losing battle. I think that down deep they do too.

As for me, I am looking forward to the Eternal Life that extends beyond the grave. Having "died" from a cardiac arrest in an ambulance, on the way to Fannin Regional Hospital on February 23, 1995, I personally know about the feeling of "peace that passes all understanding"." To be able to watch a Paramedic and an EMT work to bring me back to life and hear every word they said while clinically dead is something you can never forget. There is something more that I am not including but that is between me and God. What a wonderful experience! I spent several days in CCU but He kept His promise! I am still here after 20 years. However, I am glad the earthly end is in sight because I know what is coming. It is grand!

The next problem in our facility that needs to be rectified is the kitchen situation. When Trinka Davis Veterans Village CLC was designed it included a kitchen for each of the four "Houses" that can be viewed by residents from the dining table. The idea appears to be that it would help give that "homey" touch and to some extent it does. The kitchen contains two refrigerators (one for residents and one for the Chef), a double oven, and two sanitizers that will sanitize dishes, only after all food particles are removed and they have been washed in a small, double sink. There are cabinets and adequate counter space, which seems appropriate and a small storage room for various food items. "Homey", yes. Practical for the job that needs to be done? Not on your life!

In C-House alone, we have four diabetics who require "special diets"." In addition, we have residents with renal failure, high cholesterol and other medical issues that could suffer serious health problems from continuously eating certain kinds of foods, especially those food items containing too much protein, carbohydrates, salt, or other harmful ingredients. Only a dietician can understand and correctly recommend what foods these individuals should consume to maintain a healthy lifestyle. There is no way that these "special diets" can be prepared by a single Chef, on the equipment that is installed, in each of the four kitchens. As a result, the diet presently provided here for the residents is a "regular diet", high in protein, carbohydrates, and salt. Tasty? Sometimes. Good for residents with specific medical problems that require "special diets" to prevent the decline of their medical problems? You must be kidding! An improper diet constantly fed to a person with a serious medical problem can be both harmful and life shortening!

The solution for this problem, in my opinion, is simple as it applies to the planning and construction of the next facility similar to Trinka Davis Veterans Village. The Community Living Center portion of the building should have a large main kitchen where Chefs can work as a team to cook both regular and special diets. It should be equipped with proper cook stoves that contain an adequate number of burners to prepare several different food items simultaneously. The main kitchen should also be equipped with proper dishwashers and sterilizing equipment as well as a large walk in freezer and sufficient storage space to keep food and supplies. Prepared food should be placed in steam carts to keep food hot and taken to the several "Houses" for distribution to the residents. These steam carts are electrically heated and be purchased retail for $2000.00 or less each. In other words, use roughly the same food preparation methods as the average hospital.

The original idea of making the "Houses" seem more "homelike" by having separate kitchens in each one should be retained, at least in part. While the stoves and sterilizers could be eliminated, the large refrigerators should remain. The idea of one refrigerator for residents and the other for general use is a good one. The inclusion of a storage area, similar to the existing small storage room in the present facility, could be used for snack foods and other items and served to the residents by CNAs. The coffee makers and a microwave plus paper plates and cups would eliminate any need for a dishwasher and could be disposed of in large trash containers. The tables and chairs should remain. Collectively, they would retain that feeling of "Home" for residents which appears to have been the original idea.

As to a solution to the existing "four kitchen" situation in Trinka Davis Veterans Village CLC using one or more of the existing kitchens for preparation of "special diets" and the remaining kitchens for "regular diets" would help solve the problem. "Special diet" foods could be delivered in steam carts to residents in the various "Houses" who require them and placed on the tables in the appropriate places. This would retain the original atmosphere without much additional cost. I am sure the rough ideas I have proposed could be greatly improved on by professionals in the field but change is definitely needed to make the dining experience healthier for residents with "special needs"."

That about winds up my suggestions as to the changes I personally believe would improve the Community Living Center portion of Trinka Davis Veterans Village. Most are comparatively minor and would add little cost to the construction of this part of this facility or others like it that might be built in the future. In comparison to construction projects, under supervision of the Department of Veterans Affairs, which typically require numerous expensive changes, run an average of thirty five months late and nearly always over budget, Trinka Davis Veterans Village was a miracle! But then it was built with private money, planned with the help of a very qualified architect, constructed by a first rate contractor and then donated to the Veterans Administration.

As to modifications that are necessary to improve usability of the Outpatient Clinic portions of future facilities like ours, and to more efficiently serve both veterans and staff, some fairly expensive changes would be required. Those changes would be much cheaper to install during original construction rather than in trying to install them after the building had been constructed, which in some instances can prove prohibitively expensive or next to impossible! As a Master Electrician, and former electrical contractor, who has done it both ways, I speak from personal experience.

The first improvement concerns the treatment rooms. I have had to go into some of them and they are simply too small. Trying to get into the Podiatrist's or the Dentist's chairs is extremely difficult for someone who is wheelchair bound. The solution is to increase the size of treatment rooms on future facilities by about two feet in width and two feet in length. As to our current facility, there is no simple solution. Attempting to enlarge what already exists would prove to be prohibitively expensive. We will probably need to continue to use these rooms just as they are. It may be that some unexpected medical services were added, after construction, and the required space for them was not anticipated. Should an additional building be constructed at Trinka Davis Veterans Village to provide more extensive outpatient services for area veterans and CLC residents' adequate space for treatment rooms should be a major consideration.

I also suggest that in future construction of facilities

similar to Trinka Davis Veterans Village sufficient space for a CT scanner, ultrasound equipment and echocardiograms should be included as a part of the original plan. This would allow "on site" physicians to screen veteran patients locally instead of sending them to a distant Veterans Medical Center to access those same services. It would result in more timely diagnostic services, eliminate much of the distant travel for veterans, reduce "wait time" to obtain appointments for the same kind of services at crowded VA Medical Centers and, in my opinion, be extremely cost effective. There would be no need for a costly MRI at these smaller facilities as the CT scanner can produce sufficient results for most diagnostic purposes. Any surgery, beyond the most minor procedures, as well as all major diagnostic procedures including colonoscopies and endoscopies, should be performed at major VA Medical Centers where unexpected problems that may develop during the procedure can be more effectively dealt with.

I personally believe it would be productive if a number of medical specialties at these minor facilities were added such as orthopedics, gastroenterology, dermatology, and such other medical modalities as might prove practical. These services could be provided on either a "full" or "part time" basis according to the needs of the particular facility. Using the smaller Outpatient Clinic facilities to treat less serious medical issues and for pre-screening and referring major medical problems to VA Medical Centers, as required, would reduce "patient load" and improve "patient treatment access time"." It would also leave the VA Medical Centers freer to treat the more complex medical and surgical problems on a timely basis and save money for taxpayers by reducing travel and a number of other costs.

Today we had a Fire Drill that didn't happen. What actually did happen was so comical that many of us in C-House, nearly split a gut laughing ourselves silly. It was one of those typical VA screw ups that have both a "humorous side" and make no sense at all. A number of us were seated at the breakfast table at shortly before seven am drinking juice and coffee while we waited for Mack to begin cooking breakfast. We got a tipoff that a Fire Drill would be held at seven fifteen and, since it was so cold, we would be huddling in the hall instead of being forced to go outside to freeze our collective backsides off. Our suite doors were closed and locked up tight by a CNA (who shall remain "nameless") and we readied ourselves for the big moment when the fire bell began to flash and scream out its annoying sound.

Seven fifteen came and went and nothing happened! C.B., my eighty nine year old next door neighbor, needed to use his bathroom but had to "hold it" as he had been "locked out of his suite"." He scrooched around in his chair at the table, grimaced and held on as best he could. Seven thirty came and still no Fire Alarm. Mack, the Chef, gave up and started to cook our breakfast of pancakes, eggs, and (in my case) pork sausage. About seven forty five Mack set it on the table. Not knowing when, or if, the darn thing would go off, I ate rapidly. It was easy for me, having once lived in Granny Raley's boarding house where, if you hoped for "seconds", you had to be quick!

Eight o'clock arrived. Still nothing. No flashing lights, no clanging alarm. Finally, at about eight fifteen, the staff started to unlock the doors to our suites and quietly announced the Fire Drill had been cancelled. C.B. grabbed his rolling walker and made a mad dash for his suite, his cheeks puffed out and his eyes in a squint. When he returned there was a look of relief on his face. A few minutes later we collectively rose from the table and returned to our quarters. And that is the story of the Fire Drill that never happened! I wonder what the VA has planned for us next? Nothing would surprise me after seeing some of the antics that go on around here! But at least it keeps you laughing and on your toes.

One more thing that comes to mind is somewhat pitiful and hilarious. It is the bed sheets! The beds we sleep in are about 48 inches wide and 80 inches long somewhere between the size of a twin and a double. I guess they are what you could call an extra-long three quarter bed, or there about. When I first came here, about eight months ago, there were no sheets that would fit our beds so the CNAs were forced use an extra-long flat double sheet and tie all four ends so they could use it as sort of a fitted sheet. The knots had to be done exactly right. If they were tied too tight they could let go in the middle of the night and you would find yourself sleeping on the bottom blue plastic pad that is installed around the mattress to keep it from getting soiled in case the occupant has an accident. Another extra-long double flat sheet was used for the top. Not too bad.

This "tie knots in the sheet" plan worked, sort of. There were only a few of the CNAs that had the proper sheet tying knack so surprises happened regularly. I would always try to have Juanita Kirk or Nikki Morris change my sheets as they were expert at it and I could sleep through the night feeling fairly safe from "blue plastic" midnight surprise, Then along came Teresa Easter, another proper knot maker, and I had one more CNA I could count on. Things went along fairly well for several months until someone in the VA came up with a new idea as to how to replace the current bed sheet method. As usual, it was a disaster! And that is putting it mildly!

The extra-long double sheets were replaced with a queen sized bottom fitted sheet and a queen size (or larger) top sheet. This is probably the stupidest idea anyone ever had but it is about par for some of the whacky ideas the VA seems to occasionally come up with. The queen bottom fitted sheet is so oversized for the small bed that it is full of wrinkles. Uncomfortable to sleep on? You have got to be kidding! As for the queen (or larger) top sheet, it hangs down so far on both sides that it kisses the floor! Some of the CNAs tuck it in around the mattress and trying to pull it out so you can get under the sheets is enough to drive you out of your mind! A fitting punishment for the ding bat who came up with this silly plan would be to shove him under these oversize wrinkly sheets, strap him down tightly and make him spend a week wrapped in his own idea. Kind of cruel? Yeah!

An unusual thing happened at breakfast a couple of days ago. W. J. got over his "snit" against the VA! He came to the table with a smile on his face stating the battle against, what he considered, stupid VA regulations that were depriving him of his constitutional rights was over and he had decided to stay in C-House. I have no idea as to whether he acquiesced and gave in to accepting help to fill his bird feeders, or if he decided to remove them. Anyway, he is back to his sometimes happy, sometimes grouchy, old self and meals at the table have become pleasant once again. W.J. actually enjoys going out of his way to help others and he is very good at it. I think he has probably been that way most of his life and that is one of the reasons I chose him for a friend. At ninety five years of age he is still very sharp as a tack and his mind is clear as a bell. Maybe a little "bull headed" at times but aren't we all?

I have been a resident of C-House, in Trinka Davis Veterans Village Community Living Center for just over a year. I came here deeply depressed; nearly blind; suffering from chronic pain; diabetes; kidney failure; a host of other medical issues and with no desire to live. And within the first couple of weeks a hypertensive crisis almost gave me my wish. After I recovered, I began to examine Trinka Davis Veterans Village, traveling its length and breadth, inside and outside via power wheelchair. I soon began to realize what a magnificent and amazing "one of a kind" facility it was. I began to understand my purpose in being here was to tell the story of Trinka Davis Veterans Village Community Living Center, its residents and its staff. I began to talk with both residents and staff and listen to their life stories. I developed questionnaires for both residents and staff to gain correct information to be able to tell their stories exactly as they happened. Since I was nearly blind, I started writing with a powerful magnifying glass.

I started off by telling my own story and when that was complete I queried residents as to what they did while in the military; the theaters where they had served and how they had received their disabilities. To a man they gave me, truthful straight and detailed answers. Some had held the information about how they had become service disabled within themselves and had never discussed it with anyone since the day it happened. I believe they told me their stories without embellishment because they realized I had been there, done that and had also walked those same miles in their moccasins. I tried to honor each one as I wrote. These were men who had unselfishly served our country and, like me, had paid a high price in serious lifelong disabilities for the privilege. Just to be eligible for admission to VA nursing facilities, like Trinka Davis Veterans Village CLC, requires that the veteran have received at least a seventy percent service incurred disability. Most here are rated at one hundred percent. And everyone who lives here would step up again to answer our country's call even if they knew in advance they would end up like they have. They put love of country before self! My next task was to query the staff and discover their life stories and what had motivated them to come to work at Trinka Davis Veterans Village, CLC. Their questionnaire was somewhat different from the one I had developed for the residents and sought to learn about their families, their educational background and their prior work experience. I found out two very important facts, many of them were themselves veterans or family members of veterans and several of them were service disabled. Almost to a person, their reason for coming here was to help veterans. Talk about dedication! They have it in spades and it shows in the caring way they do their jobs. In the months I have been living here they have become like my second family!

As I continued to write "JUST BEFORE TAPS", I had a number of very serious medical issues occur. I fell to the floor of my suite three times; had a mini-stroke; more serious hypertensive crises and the worsening of my kidney failure I began to wonder if I would live long enough to finish my story. I also had a stroke of good fortune. Thanks to successful surgery, I recovered the sight in my right eye and was able to write without the use of my magnifying glass. Somehow I knew I would live to finish my book because I believed my purpose in being put here was to write it.

I also believe that if you put your mind to it and never

give up, you can do almost anything you set out to do. I do not believe in the "I am a victim" mentality as an excuse for setting on your haunches and accomplishing nothing. The answer is to "never give up if things go wrong" and do not accept "I can't" for a copout! If an 87 year old, one hundred percent service disabled veteran; with one eye, diabetes; hypertension; renal failure; severe spinal stenosis; a brain tumor and neuropathy in both legs, like me, can type an entire book with just one finger, tell me, just what is your excuse for sitting around and doing nothing? And with that little pearl of wisdom I will end my story! I hope you enjoy reading it as much as I enjoyed telling it.

GW and Cinnamon

EPILOGUE

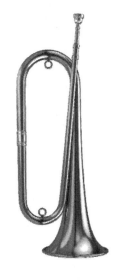

WHY I WROTE
"JUST BEFORE TAPS"

When I first came to Trinka Davis Veterans Village Community Living Center, on May 15, 2014. I had absolutely no intention of writing anything. I came here to die! Severely depressed after years of disability, severe pain, rapidly declining health, and mostly confined to a power wheelchair, I also had a prosthetic left eye. My right eye was 20/150 which left me with greatly diminished sight. I was nearly blind. My wife of forty seven years, Jeanne, was suffering from memory problems and had been diagnosed with vascular dementia. We had finally reached a point where we could no longer take care of each other. Something had to be done.

I am a 100 percent service connected disabled WWII veteran, rated permanent and total since January, 1963. For the past year, the Veterans Administration had furnished me with Home Health Care three days a week three hours a day. It helped, but based on the seriousness of the medical problems Jeanne and I had developed, it simply wasn't enough. I was eighty six years old, Jeanne was eighty three. With the help of Doctors Rina Eisenstein and Regina Sherman plus Social Workers, Mrs. Lerch, at Atlanta VAMC, and Jennifer Talley, at Trinka Davis Veterans Village, arrangements were made for me to become a resident of C-House. With assistance from our daughter, Julie Shannon, my wife Jeanne was moved the same day to an apartment at Emeritus Riverstone Assisted Living, in Canton, Georgia along with our cat, Snoopy, as her "live in" companion. We no longer lived together.

As I stated in my first paragraph, I came here to die and during the first couple of weeks I almost did! After I improved somewhat with the help of Dr. Jamya Pittman and the staff I began to look around the facility where I was going to spend what time I had left. What I discovered was that Trinka Davis Veterans Village, was "one of a kind" in the whole United States. It offers a private suite with bath, a nursing staff that gives incomparable care, a choice of daily activities, volunteer groups that come constantly to help improve the quality of life, and an attached Outpatient Clinic that not only serves the area's veteran population but residents as well. And none of this would have been possible except for the generosity of Trinka Davis and the Foundation she created. Amazing!

I decided this was a story that needed to be told and I wanted to be the one to tell it. Tell it to the people of our nation about the wonderful living conditions, the great nursing care, and all the amenities that make life for seriously service disabled veterans worth living. Not a place like some of the current facilities where two disabled veterans had to share a crowded room and a single toilet and shower with two more disabled veterans living in the adjacent crowded room! Maybe if I was able to tell the story of Trinka Davis Veterans Village well enough someone who read it would follow the example set by Trinka Davis and the Foundation she created. And maybe...just maybe...if they were patriots who had been blessed with success in life they would step up to create another miracle like she did! It was worth a shot!

I had some experience at writing but I had never attempted to write anything like this. Besides, I was in extremely poor health and could hardly see...certainly not well enough for such an overwhelming task! I thought about it day after day. Suddenly, the title "JUST BEFORE TAPS" popped into my head as appropriate for the story because for most of us living here our next stop would be the cemetery where the mournful sound of "TAPS" would be played as we were laid to rest. It was then that I decided to try to tell the story of Trinka Davis Veterans Village. As I could barely see I began to write the book with the help of a powerful magnifying glass. That was the only way I could know what I was writing. It was slow! But things were about to get better.

In July, 2014, about a month and a half after I came to live here, I had cataract surgery on my remaining eye, at Atlanta VA Medical Center. At a service in our Trinka Davis Veterans Village Chapel, just prior to my surgery, I had asked the Chaplain, Reverend Monique Jimmerson, and the residents who were present to pray for me. They did! The doctors at the VA Eye Clinic where I had been treated over the years had held out little hope for me to regain much of my vision, due to macular degeneration and retinal scarring, Amazingly, thanks to God and the skill of Dr. Douglas Blackmon, I came out of surgery with almost perfect vision. The story is detailed in my book. As I wrote, my health continued to fail. It made me wonder many times if I would live long enough to finish the story. If you are reading this...I guess I must have!

George F. Woodruff

GA PATRIOT GUARD RIDERS

Top: My Aunt Fleta Crothers & Uncle Arthur Schumaker
Grandmother in center: Mary Schumaker
Left side: My Uncle Otho Schumaker
Bottom: My mother Verda Woodruff

Top: Daughter Cheryl with son-in-law John Lewkowicz

Daughter Sandra Woodruff
with son-in-law
Thomas Richard Moreau

Dogs: Moose(the big one)
Misty (the smaller one)

Neil Shannon
(grandson)

Thomas Edward
Shannon (son-in-law)

Julie Shannon
(daughter)

Cory Shannon
(grandson)

Julie Shannon
(daughter)

Jeanne Woodruff
(wife)

Cheryl Lewkowicz
(daughter)

ACKNOWLEDGEMENTS

"JUST BEFORE TAPS" is dedicated to honoring the memory of Trinka Davis whose concern for disabled veterans made the miracle of Trinka Davis Veterans Village possible and to the Foundation she created that carried out her dream. Special thanks go to Ms. Nancy C. Hughes and Ms. Leah F. Scalise of the law firm of Hughes and Scalise, PC for their participation in making Trinka Davis Veterans Village a reality. The help and encouragement I received from these ladies in writing this book is beyond price. They deserve the eternal gratitude of we seriously disabled veterans whose lives here have been made better by providing us with a home that gives our final days quality and meaning. So many other people helped with or provided inspiration for the writing of "JUST BEFORE TAPS" and it is difficult to know just where to begin to say "Thank You" for their valuable contributions and support. I will try to do it as best I can and pray that any individuals, organizations, and groups I may have overlooked will forgive me.

My sincerest appreciation goes: To: the CLC Physician In Charge, Jamya Pittman, M.D., and to Nurse Practitioner Mrs. Mamron Warner, whose medical skills and encouragement kept me functioning well enough that I was able to finish writing "JUST BEFORE TAPS"."

To: my Psychologist, Dr. Patricia Rivera, Phd, who

patiently listens to my problems and, To: her 80 pound German Shepherd Therapy Dog, Outlaw, who flops on my bed intent on providing me with much appreciated doggy companionship.

To: Trinka Davis Veterans Village CLC's Clinical Social Worker Jennifer Talley who pushed me around the Community Living Center in a wheelchair when my wife, Jeanne, our daughter, Julie Shannon, and I first came to the facility to look it over prior to my admission and who has been there for me ever since.

To: the RNs, LPNs, and CNAs of C-House who cared for and put up with an irascible old scoundrel (me) thereby becoming like a "second family" and giving the remaining part of my life some real meaning.

To: the Housekeeping staff who keep our suites in C-House spotless, sugar ant, and germ free and

To: the awesome Chefs who despite numerous, loud, unjustified complaints, patiently cook our meals.

To: the Interdisciplinary Care Team Members, at Trinka Davis Veterans Village,, CLC, who meet with me quarterly to review and develop my Care Plan so I can continue to function at my best level possible.

To: the Physician Manager, Robert Norvell, M.D., and To: the Nurse Associate Manager, Dr. Connie Hampton, Phd, who are in charge of Trinka Davis Veterans Village, To: Steven Releford, MSN, CLC Nurse Manager, and to all their assistants for the fine jobs they do in helping to manage this facility.

To: our Recreational Therapists who plan the daily activities that make life better for all CLC residents and who work endlessly to see that they are carried out.

To: our many caring volunteer organizations who let us know we have not been forgotten by visiting us frequently and providing activities like Bingo games, various types of recreation, tasty meals, welcome Christmas gifts, and enjoyable companionship including American Legion Post 143 in Carrollton; Post 264 in Mableton; Post 145 in Douglasville; Post 294 in Powder Springs; Post 70 in Villa Rica; the AMVETs; the Patriot Guard Riders of Georgia; the Friends of Trinka Davis; Soldier's Angels and the numerous other volunteers who come here often to freely give of their time and talents. You make our lives more livable. Thank You!

To: all the residents of "A", "B", and "C" Houses (now and in the future) who have become seriously disabled while proudly serving our country and have willingly paid a high price for that honor.

To: our lady Master barber, Jerri Williams, who comes here regularly to cut the hair of those who still have some left and to sympathize with those who don't. And she does it all without charge! Bless you Jerri!

To Deacon Judith Kalom, of St. Clements Episcopal Church, in Canton, GA, and to her husband, Peter, who have faithfully made the 140 mile trip to visit and bring me Holy Communion.

To David Ray, of Mineral Bluff, GA, a true and longtime friend whose sharp eyesight and skill in editing made "JUST BEFORE TAPS" much more readable.

And with all my love To: my beloved and multi-talented daughter Sandra Woodruff, R.D. who encouraged me as I wrote "JUST BEFORE TAPS" and who has written several bestselling books on healthy diets and healthy living, and To: my beloved, intelligent and always dependable daughter, Julie Shannon, who looks after her mother's (my dear wife, Jeanne) interests and brings her here to visit me frequently. And . . . To: my entire family...my wife, my beautiful daughters, my beloved step daughter, Cheryl, my three lucky sons-in-law, and my two usually adult grandsons, Neil and Cory. You are my family! Without you, life would have had little meaning! You are, and forever will be, my pride and joy!

ABOUT THE AUTHOR

George Woodruff is 87 years old. He has been a resident of C-House, at Trinka Davis Veterans Village Community Living Center in Carrollton, Georgia, since May 15, 2014. A 100 percent service disabled veteran with disabilities that have been rated as Permanent and Total since January, 1963, he is a diabetic, suffers from hypertension, has a non-malignant brain tumor, a complex partial seizure disorder, a prosthetic left eye, serious renal failure, severe stenosis in his lower back, and neuropathy in both legs and feet. His current method of transportation is a power wheelchair.

George served in two different branches of the military, the U. S. Navy during World War II, (1944-45) and in the U. S. Army (1947-50). He was medically discharged from the Army's Brooke General Hospital in San Antonio, Texas, on September 14, 1950, shortly after the Korean War began. In addition to lengthy in-patient hospitalizations in Military

Hospitals in both Germany and the United States during his time in service, George was hospitalized in eight different VA Medical Centers for a total of 26 times over nearly 70 years. In spite of his medical issues he managed to build a solid record of accomplishments which he believes could never have happened without the help of Almighty God.

George served as a Campaign Strategist, Political Consultant, and Legislative Advisor for nearly 40 years. He has an extensive background in speech writing, campaign literature design, TV and radio spot composition, and direct mail advertising. He managed candidate and issue campaigns in Florida, Georgia, and North Carolina. During the 1970's, as Publicity Chairman of the Brevard County, Florida, Republican Party, he drafted a "Campaign Code of Ethics" that was adopted by both political parties. In 1991, he was appointed by Rep. Everett A. Kelly the Speaker Pro Tem of the Florida House to participate in the Collins Center For Public Policy's Convening, in Tallahassee, and aided in the development and state level acceptance of Florida's first Voluntary Code of Fair Campaign Practices. In 1997-98, he served as Secretary of the Fannin County, Georgia, Republican Party.

During the late 1970's, George served as a Consultant to the Christian Action League of North Carolina. In 1979 he was appointed by church leaders to serve as Executive Director of the multi-denominational Concerned Citizens for a Better Asheville and Buncombe County. He has worked for the creation of Drug Task Forces in both North Carolina and Florida. Between the years of 1969 and 1977, as President of St. Mark's Eight, Inc., George made numerous trips to Colombia, South America, seeking government permission to conduct an underwater salvage operation off the Caribbean coast of that country. With the help of friends in the Roman Catholic Church, he successfully negotiated the first permit ever issued by the Colombian government to allow the salvage of treasure from sunken Spanish galleons. During an extended 1977 trip, at the request of a Florida Congressman, George developed information and prepared an on-site Confidential Report describing methods used by illegal drug suppliers to maintain the Cocaine-Marijuana flow from Colombia to the United States. He also served as a Director of the Kennedy Memorial Fund of Colombia along with prominent members of the Roman Catholic Clergy and the wife of the country's former President.

George has an extensive record of service to veterans and military organizations. He represented the Florida Commander's Conference consisting of nine veteran and military organizations before the Florida State Legislature and served as State Resolutions Chairman and State Legislative Officer for the Disabled American Veterans, Dept. of Florida. He also served for four years as a member of a Florida Congressional District Military Academy Selection Committee under former Congressman Buddy McKay. After moving to Georgia he served as State Legislative Co-Chairman for the Disabled American Veterans, Dept. of Georgia, and for two years as a Member of a Panel charged with assisting in the selection of Military Academy appointees for former Georgia Congressman Ed Jenkins.

George Woodruff was born in Avilla, Indiana, to George Henry Woodruff and Verda Schumaker Woodruff, on July 29, 1927. He moved to Florida from Akron, Ohio, in 1946, and later to Fannin County, Georgia, in 1987. George has been a Master Mason since 1954, is a Knight Templar, a member of the American Legion, and a Life Member of the Disabled American Veterans.

He has previously written two works of Christian fiction "DAY OF INDIGNATION" (1996) and "MIRACLE AT ST. LUKE'S" (2002). Both were set in the north Georgia Mountains. George has been in a wonderful loving, marriage for over 47 years. His wife Jeanne, who suffers from memory problems, lives in Brookdale Assisted Living, in Canton, Georgia, near their daughter, Julie Shannon. George and Jeanne are members of St. Clements Episcopal Church, in Canton, Georgia.

CREDITS

"While I did not use any direct excerpts from the book "Trinka Davis: Southern by Choice", I did receive a great deal of inspiration and valuable information from reading about the life story of Trinka Davis, her vision to accomplish something of significance that would both honor and serve veterans in need of assistance, and would also give back to the small communities in western Georgia that had given such friendship and loyalty to her, I feel duty bound to assign proper credit, and to fulfill my request for permission to quote from the book made to Nancy Hughes of the Trinka Davis Foundation, which she graciously granted along with a great deal of valuable help from both Ms. Hughes and Ms. Leah Scalise. "Thank you."

While every attempt has been made to provide a view of the life of Trinka and her family, [Trinka Davis: Southern by Choice"] is based on anecdotal and informational research. It should not be taken as authoritative or definitive.

True Stories of Courage, Faith, and Healing.

An Anthology By Lemon Press

Made in the USA
Charleston, SC
04 January 2016